Cultivating U
within the
Biodiversity of God

Cultivating Unity within the Biodiversity of God

Anne Primavesi

POLEBRIDGE PRESS
Salem, Oregon

Cover art by Glynn Gorick glynn@gorick.co.uk
Layout and interior design by Robaire Ream

Library of Congress Cataloging-in-Publication Data
Primavesi, Anne, 1934-
   Cultivating unity within the biodiversity of God / Anne Primavesi.
      p. cm.
   Includes bibliographical references (p.   ) and index.
   ISBN 978-1-59815-031-5 (alk. paper)
   1. Human ecology--Religious aspects--Christianity. 2. Biodiversity.
3. Jesus Christ. 4. God (Christianity) 5. Kingdom of God.
6. Theology. I. Title.
   BT695.5.P743 2011
   261.8′8--dc23
                                                        2011026023

CONTENTS

FOREWORD

When all things began, the Word already was.
The Word dwelt with God, and what God was, the
Word was. The Word, then, was with God at the
beginning, and through him all things came to be;
no single thing was created without him.
—John 1:1–3

In 1998 the United Nations Environment Programme published a major complementary contribution to its Global Biodiversity Assessment (GBA) entitled *Cultural and Spiritual Values of Biodiversity*. This document was commissioned when it was noted that in the GBA, whereas scientists take for granted that as a "form of life" we are an integral and critically important part of global biodiversity, there was a religious and cultural tendency to treat the human species as separate from the rest of nature. And as we are the dominant influence on biodiversity, there is a need to improve our understanding of our place within it.[1]

Implicit in this statement is the fact that we are *not* separate from the rest of nature. While the concept of biodiversity was unknown to the Christian(s) of the first and early second century CE, such as those who wrote the opening passage in the gospel of John cited above, they grasped the sacred unity that permeates existence as a whole. Within that whole there has been a diversity of life forms since "all things began." That is the originating moment of the terrestrial biodiversity created and sustained by God within whose unity we are sustained as one particular life form. Biodiversity is integral to our being alive. And therefore, perhaps, to God being alive for us.

1

Dieter Hessel quotes Mark Wallace:

> God is so internally related to the universe
> That . . . to wreak environmental havoc
> on the earth is to run the risk that we
> will do irreparable
> even fatal harm to the Mystery we call God.[2]

At the close of the Year of Biodiversity (2010), the 170 countries of the United Nations Environment Program that have signed the Convention on Biodiversity designated 2011–2022 the Decade of Biodiversity. Its focus is on the fact that our interrelatedness not only has a global dimension but that the relationships between the individual and the global environment work at the personal level also. Planetary unity between life-form and ecosystem is sustained by the interrelatedness of life (including ours) at all levels of biological diversity. Quite simply, our individual well-being is inextricably linked to the well-being of the whole.

Therefore personally cultivating unity within the whole consciously links our own well-being with that of *"all things that have come to be"* and, ultimately, with the God through whom planetary biodiversity came to be. It is easy to say this, but as we know, to live accordingly requires a change in our perception not only of what constitutes the good of the whole but also of the God who is creating that whole. How then can we claim that this God is concerned only with the good of the human community? And if not, how are we to change the ways in which we deal individually and collectively with our species' involvement in the ever-increasing loss of biodiversity? For the most part, this is the result of human population growth, our mass migration to cities, ongoing political, economic, and religious disputes, and their escalation into armed conflicts. As all these destroy the habitats of both human and non-human creatures, they must be seen as *visible violence done to bio-*

logical diversity. And whether or not we willingly or directly inflict poverty, war, or ecological degradation on others, ultimately we all suffer from their effects and have to deal with them.

Changing our ways as nonviolently as possible calls for a rejection of violence in all its forms. It precludes people being subjugated, repressed, coerced, or exploited through a lack of respect for the diversity of their genetic, cultural, environmental or religious inheritance. Implicitly or explicitly, this dedication to nonviolence is based on whether or not we take biodiversity seriously. For the impulse to inflict harm on other life forms is best inhibited by a recognition and appreciation of the intrinsic value of their diverse gifts and of different cultural, religious, and personal perspectives.

᠙᠊

Against this contemporary background I shall look at some of the ways in which our Christian inheritance has contributed to or limited our respect for biodiversity. Within that inheritance we find a belief in the oneness of God and in the unity of Word and God—as well as different responses to it. Acknowledging this truth as openly as possible may help cultivate religious unity at a time when disunity between religions is the basis for appalling violence against people and their environments. At the same time, the unity of global well-being is increasingly threatened by the loss of species, of their habitats, and of their genetic diversity.

Taken together, these forms of violence raise vital questions for those of us with a Christian background. Is our common perception of God at variance with Jesus' own understanding of our Father's "kingdom"? Would a better appreciation of the God of Jesus inspire us to cultivate unity through reverence for diversity? Would such a perception encourage us to act in a way conducive to the long-term, universal reduction of violence? How do we respond to the fact that Jesus suffered a violent death but did not inflict violence on any living being? Do we, like the gospel writers, perceive him as fulfilling the prophecy of one sent by God as a messenger of peace: not contentious nor loud-mouthed, not one to break a bruised reed or extinguish a sputtering flame (Isaiah 42:1–4)?

Any religious attempt today to express our earthly unity occurs under the aegis of scientific narratives that often have as their (unspoken) presupposition our unity within the diverse community of life on Earth. Yet, though science makes no claims about our unity with God, its assertions about our shared origins with other species and shared dependence on global ecosystems are often resisted and even dismissed on the grounds that we are different from all other beings in both degree and kind.

Underlying this resistance is a sense of human special-ness, long fostered by philosophy as well as religion, that presumes us to be intellectually and morally superior to all other creatures. This has been accepted to such an extent that the humanism found within western culture often amounts to worship of humanity. Several of its exponents, such as Auguste Comte and Julian Huxley, have explicitly promoted it as a religion.[3]

When Christians assert human uniqueness, it is usually on the same grounds but with the added claim that God became "one of us" in Jesus. Underlying both claims may be the understandable feeling that we have quite enough to do looking after ourselves without being responsible for the welfare—or the demise—of the whole earthly commu-nity. This resistance becomes even stronger as our aware-ness of the realities of global climate change increases and along with it a reluctance to be involved in solving the problems it brings. For while climate change makes it increasingly difficult for us to deny our "oneness" with all other beings, it also calls for taking steps to deal with its implications that affect our lifestyles.

◯◯

A more promising scientific route to cultivating unity is to ask a very different question: *When* did "all things" begin? Thanks to modern cosmological physics, we can date our universe back some 13.7 billion years and the evolution of our solar system to just under five billion years. Our confident calculation of such answers relies on our presuming a pre-existing unity between us, all life on earth, and the universe as a whole. For we know that we began to evolve only when everything required for the emergence of our species had already evolved: this includes fresh air, clean water, fertile soil, the right amount of solar energy, abundant plant life, and a long ancestry of pre-human living beings.

Geologists agree that Cambrian fossils found on the South Coast of England and in the Burgess Shale of the Canadian Rockies suggest an explosion of animal life on the planet about five hundred million years ago. Evolutionary biologists accept that our first direct ancestors, the earliest examples of *homo sapiens,* began to appear about half a million years ago. Their emergence was intrinsically connected to and depended on all those living beings that appeared before then. As does our existence today.

This timeline tracing our "beginning" is usually presented in horizontal form, starting at the point furthest backward in time and continuing on into the present day. A more precise but much more complex vertical model would display our "beginnings" as a series of layers or deposits revealed in increasing number and depth. Or to create an even more relevant and revealing display, we could turn the whole thing around, placing those most remote in time out in front of us and those yet to come stretched out behind us, dependent for their survival on what we leave for them.

Catherine Keller captures this truth brilliantly:

> "We are created from *everything*," exclaims a friend, gazing at his newborn child. He is thinking of the dust of stars, species and genes, of histories and personalities, recycled in this unpredictable little *nova*, folded like a bud in his arms.[4]

Earth's past in all its forms lies before us as an essential, unifying presence in our lives that we help to recycle into the unpredictable future of those coming after us. This unity in time gives us a wider perspective, a more comprehensive viewpoint from which to explore and symbolize our unity in being. Today we can and do speak about the impact of human lives and lifestyles evident in their present and future effects: loss of habitat, extinction of species, destruction of natural resources, and rising temperatures. We are reluctantly aware of their already devastating impact on particular human groups and on the variety of creatures sustained (or not) by the affected environments.

୬୦

All of this raises fundamental religious questions for Christian and non-Christian alike: What role have mythic visions of God played in human history? Is it not fair to say that in those which have influenced and been influenced by Christianity, the divine gaze appears focused on one particular species, the human? Have we erred in our assumption that we alone are capable of knowing or responding to that gaze? A further and specifically Christian assumption concerns when and how "all things" began. The Genesis narrative that informed the author(s) of the gospel of John opens on a stage that is empty except for an almighty creator God who, "when all things began," brought each species into existence by the power of "his" word. This God continues to be envisioned and hymned as the "One God, Lord of heaven and earth and of all things, visible and invisible."

That fundamentally male image of a God with absolute power, existing outside of earthly time and history, and bringing all forms of life into existence, is deeply-rooted and vividly expressed in many religious traditions, rituals, myths, symbols, and philosophies. It has provided answers to, or rather, has forestalled any questions about how "all things" began by identifying God as a transcendent power—one with the ability to begin (and/or end) the lives of all members of the community of life on Earth.

Particular aspects of this powerful mythic image were embedded in Jewish, Christian, and pagan religious traditions extant in the Roman Empire during the first century CE. They served as the ultimate and present referent for the myth of imperial power and its cult, or *koinon*: one cultivated and promoted in various ways, but most widely and successfully through coins bearing Caesar's image with the legend *"Divi Filius"* (Son of God). Since the Christianization of the Roman Empire in the fourth century CE, or more accurately, the imperial Romanization of Christianity, religious imagination and rituals have consistently identified the God of Jesus with such totalitarian power.

Jesus, too, as "Word made flesh," has been identified as "the Christ"—a Messiah or Savior with this kind of power. Murals and paintings of him as *Pantocrator*—all-powerful creator, king and judge—adorn churches, basilicas, and cathedrals, all of which are themselves emblematic of imperial power exercised by ecclesiastical rulers. The clear message behind these images is that the only possible relationship between us and him is that of absolute obedience on our part, a situation Paul expressed vividly in cosmic terms:

> Therefore God has highly exalted him and bestowed on him the name which is above every name, that at the name of Jesus every knee should bow, in heaven and on earth and under the earth, and every tongue confess that Jesus Christ is Lord, to the glory of God the Father. (Philippians 2:10)

Yet, while human knees have bowed and human tongues confessed these mythic biblical images of God and of Jesus, within those same biblical sources we find Jesus and the prophets directly challenging them. The clearest and perhaps most effective modes of dissent were and are allegorical narratives and parables, the function of which within the Hebrew Bible and in the records of Jesus' life and teaching is to question the myths attached to and supporting imperial images of God. In fact, Jesus' actions and teaching directly contradict those myths that supported not only Egyptian, Assyrian, Greek, and Roman imperial rule, but also Jewish belief in the sacred power of God to destroy their totalitarian oppressors.

Thankfully, very few such "absolute powers" remain to be mythically invoked, nor does avowed political support of slavery exist. But the mythic power of global financial systems has been starkly revealed by a world recession and by the evident desire of governments and individuals alike to support these systems or share in their profits, all the while attempting to cloak the fact that their mechanisms thrive by fostering greed and financial disunity, by accumulating material possessions and investing our security in and for monetary gain alone. These "securities" are bought only through the commodification and depletion of the Earth's resources while their exploitation for financial profit is ignored. Likewise overlooked is the consequent destruction of indigenous communities, the exploitation inherent in cheap labor and the ravaging of land and marine habitats. This means that the poor today are as much slaves of politico-economic oppression as were those overtly bought and sold in Caesar's time.

Nor is this slavery enforced and supported by financial systems alone. While we no longer have imperial legions raising or destroying fortifications, establishing border controls, and enslaving whole populations, we do have a military-industrial complex under the control of powerful nations that possess and manufacture the most sophisticated weapons of mass destruction ever made, instruments of death that implicitly threaten the life of the whole earthly community. Their range is no longer circumscribed by either the continental boundaries of Europe, Asia, and Africa, or the ambitions of Jerusalem, Rome, or Constantinople. Potential areas of conflict over decreasing resources now include the Americas, the West Indies, the whole of the Southern hemisphere, and all the surrounding oceans. Global colonization has brought indigenous peoples with their lands and wildlife to the brink of extinction. Most startling, perhaps, is the drive to expand and colonize "space" and beyond, venturing into a continually evolving "multiverse," which in biblical times only God inhabited.

These ever-expanding dimensions to human power challenge and threaten the community of life on Earth in different ways as cultures and social development both build on and reveal them. Their unifying presence is symbolized and realized in global communication and imaging systems whose design and control lie beyond the use and comprehension of the majority of those who rely on them for information and for their daily needs. Their development and use excludes other members of the community of life except as instruments controlled by us for our ends. Battery-farming, laboratory testing, and genetically modified crops are cases in point. The unacknowledged assumption that we have every right to engage in such enterprises is based either on the religious claim that God has given us the ability to do these things or, increasingly within western secular society, on the grounds that our intelligence, genes, or technologies have fitted us uniquely to seize any opportunity to exploit others.

This latter assumption is defined in the "Anthropic Principle," a thesis proposed by those who conclude that in some sense we are exempt from the checks and balances inherent in belonging to and being sustained by the whole earthly community. Such a conviction liberates its promoters from the uncomfortable feeling that perhaps the universe has purposes and aims *other* than ours.[5] Above all, it encourages the assumption already referred to: that we are the most significant form of life on earth and consequently, have rights of possession, indeed of life and death, over all others.

Contrary to the Anthropic Principle, both science and experience teach us that we are but one particular earthly life form that began to exist and can continue to thrive only *together with* "all things"—for both like them and together with them, we are involved in the process of *creating* our environments, societies, and relationships. This insight into the radical importance of biodiversity invites a commitment to cultivating a sense of our unity within biodiversity, a unity that both science and some religions teach us is already there. The term *cultivate* symbolizes all the qualities of a good gardener: unfailing attentiveness to and care for each life form with a view to the well-being of the whole. From that perspective, our common well-being is both agent and purpose of our mutual cultivation.

The creative energy this requires flows from a sensitivity to the interdependence and mutual vulnerability of the whole, and a refusal to attribute its products to any one constituent—or to God. As the baby's father realized, we are continually creating the world in which we live, and by doing so we create the future out of the past. Whether

or not we acknowledge it, whether or not we are aware of
it, we are deeply involved in the continuing cultivation or
destruction of "all things."

Therefore, our acceptance of and allegiance to the
mythic powers of the market and of the military-industrial
complexes that oppress and enslave those powerless to resist them really matters; and it matters not only to us but to
the Earth community as a whole. In this situation we need
a continuing critique of human power structures and of the
materialistic, self-centered mindset that underpins them.
Both culturally and religiously, parables challenge any image of power that legitimates human oppression of others
and the misuse of earth's resources for individualistic ends.
This function of parables will be explored at length.

With that in mind, listen to these two parables. The
first, datable to about 30 CE, comes from Jesus:

> The land of a rich man brought forth plentifully and
> he thought to himself, "What shall I do, for I have no-
> where to store my crops?" And he said, "I will do this:
> I will pull down my barns and build larger ones; and I
> will store all my grain and my goods. And I will say to
> my soul: 'Soul, you have ample goods laid up for many
> years; take your ease, eat, drink and be merry.'" But God
> said to him: "Fool! This night your soul is required of
> you, and the things you have prepared, whose will they
> be?" (Luke 12:16b–20)

The second, dated 1928, comes from the sixteen-year-old
composer John Cage, who won the Southern California
Oratorical Contest with a speech on Pan-American relations entitled "Other People Think":

> One of the greatest blessings that the United States
> could receive in the near future would be to have her
> industries halted, her business discontinued, her people
> speechless, a great pause in her world of affairs created,
> and finally to have everything stopped that runs, until

everyone should hear the last wheel go round and the last echo fade away. . . . [T]hen, in that moment of complete intermission, of undisturbed calm, would be the hour most conducive to the birth of a Pan-American Conscience.

The prescience of this speech, given the year before the Wall Street Crash and the Great Depression that followed it, resonates with the global situation today and stands as an effective critique of its causes. Biblical scholar John Dominic Crossan summarizes the parabolic message:

You have built a lovely home, myth assures us; but, whispers parable, you are right above an earthquake fault.[6]

In both instances, "hearing" parable effectively subverts the accepted vision of global security today, and by doing so raises a crucial question: What vision of world, home, or conscience are we creating or leaving behind for future generations? Answering it involves examining the myths that dominate our culture and presuppose competition, greed, and individualism as inevitable and dominant motivators for our actions and relationships. Answering it from a religious perspective—a distinction that is linguistic rather than intentional—parable helps us question the myth of an all-powerful God said to have created us (or more ruinously, his followers alone) to *inherit* the Earth rather than *inhabit* it in a manner aimed at promoting the flourishing of all its creatures.

The enduring wisdom inherent in the latter lifestyle is evident in an historic parabolic event chronicled in Plutarch's *Moralia*. Pythes, a contemporary of Xerxes, had a wise and good wife. He came by chance upon some gold mines and was delighted "not with moderation, but insatiably and beyond measure." He spent all his time there, sent the citizens down into the mines, and compelled all alike to dig or carry or wash out the gold to the exclusion of all other daily tasks. Many perished and all were exhausted.

The women then appealed to the wife of Pythes. She told them to go home and not lose heart. Then she summoned goldsmiths whom she trusted, secluded them, and ordered them to make of gold all sorts of loaves, cake, fruit and whatever else in the way of food she knew Pythes liked best.

When he arrived home and called for dinner, she had a golden table set before him that held nothing edible. Everything was made of gold. At first he was delighted, but when he had gazed his fill, he called for something to eat. She served him with a golden replica of whatever he asked for. By this time he was angry and shouted that he was hungry. Then she said, "But it is you who have created for us a plentiful supply of these things, and of nothing else. All skills in the trades have disappeared; the sowing and planting of crops has been forsaken and as no one tills the soil no food comes from it. Instead we dig and delve for useless things, wasting our own strength and that of our people."

Not surprisingly, Plutarch recorded this tale under the heading "Bravery of Women." In keeping with the social norms of his time, he identifies her only as Pythes' wife, but this cultural gap shrinks when her story is heard in the context of today's ecological awareness. Then her courageous actions become startlingly relevant. For her story exemplifies one of the enduring effects of parable. Whether by word or deed, it makes us *internalize* the effects of our actions by setting them within a larger whole: one that ultimately encompasses "all things" and our essential unity with them.

ॐ

My aim throughout this book is to draw these wide-ranging themes together as best I can.

Chapter 1 explores the account in Acts of the conversions of Cornelius and Peter, and introduces the terms *koinon* (the imperial ethos of unity imposed by force) and *koinonia* (cultivating unity peacefully in the context of our pre-existing sacred unity).

Chapter 2 introduces the narrative modes of *myth* and *parable* and their function in oral cultures. Together they act as narratives that provide both an over-arching view of life and a necessary critique of the presuppositions on which that view is based. The discussion examines the continuity between our culture and that of the gospel writers.

Chapter 3 explores how *parables* derive their meaning within the context of myth, and what happens in the transition from *oral* to *written* records. It seeks to establish connections between ancient mythological contexts and the contemporary one of climate change.

Chapter 4 shows the communicative power of *parable* in the story of Jonah and in the parables of Jesus; it is intended to serve as a way of appreciating what Jesus meant by "God's kingdom" and what that might mean for us today.

Chapter 5 discusses the metaphoric nature of myth and parable, and the way each employs its distinctive logic. Jesus himself became a parable of God in the minds of early Christians, a process that can be seen at work both in the story of his encounter with the Samaritan woman at the well and in his transformation into "the Christ."

Chapter 6 explores our self-perceptions in relation to the Earth. Considering the earth as a unity requires an acknowledgment of the negative impact of our lifestyles on the whole planetary community. This negative impact results largely from considering ourselves separate from that community and/or religiously privileged within it.

Chapter 7 details the distinctive clash between the imperial Roman *koinon* and the Father's *koinonia*. The *koinon* of Christian doctrinal unity is shown to be in conflict with the *koinonia* of Earth as understood today. This is shown through a detailed analysis of the parable of the prophet Jonah.

Chapter 8 focuses on the identification of God evidenced in the stories of Peter and Cornelius, Jonah, and Paul. This leads in turn to questioning how we identify God today and how this affects attitudes concerning our unity with the other-than-human members of the community of life.

Chapter 9 examines the account of Jesus' testing in the desert to disclose the nature of power within the *koinonia* of the Father's empire as compared to that within the *koinon* of imperial power.

Chapter 10 explores the incident in the synagogue in Nazareth where Jesus reads from Isaiah to reveal his role as a messenger of peace.

Chapter 11 focuses on love of enemies. By living according to that love, Jesus himself became a parable of God.

Chapter 12: The God revealed in Jesus is linked to Paul's conversion and Peter's message of peace.

1

CULTIVATING UNITY

And they devoted themselves to the apostles'
teaching, to cultivating unity *(koinonia)*, **to the**
breaking of bread and to prayer.
—Acts 2:42

While John was writing his Gospel and Plutarch chronicling the bravery of Pythes' wife, the author of the Acts of the Apostles was narrating the lives of Jesus' followers. It is no surprise to read that they devoted themselves to the teaching of the apostles, to the sharing of meals, and to prayer. But it may come as a surprise to find that Richard Pervo has translated the term *koinonia* as "cultivating unity". Standard translations include *fellowship* (RSV, Knox); *brotherhood* (Jerusalem Bible); *leben brüderlich zusammen* (Das Neue Testament in heutigen Deutsch); *la communion* (La Bible); or *the common life of sharing* (New English Bible; Christian Community Bible).

New Testament Greek does not support translating *koinonia* as belonging to an exclusively male body. Nor does it have the sense of the Latin *societas*. The Latin *communio*, like the French *la communion*, is nearer the mark. Being "in communion" with someone implies an activity, a shared participation in a common enterprise. *Communio* differs from *societas* in that it connotes an inward harmony, a mutual sharing, a common possessing; while *societas* means an external bond and fellowship.[1]

"Cultivating unity," however, emphasizes the positive qualities of striving for inward harmony and mutual

sharing. The critical additional element in Pervo's translation and in his commentary throughout Acts is that the
outcome of the narrated events, unity, is seen as a goal
to be actively and unremittingly pursued rather than one
that can be achieved once and for all. It is also clear that
unity applies not only to relationships within the apostolic
community, but even more to relationships between it and
the larger society. This, as we shall see, required a complete
reversal in their perception of who "belongs" to it, and
therefore of how and with whom they themselves are to
be united. In fact it calls for a radical reassessment of their
understanding of God and consequently of their community identity and practice. At a personal level it requires a
commitment that fundamentally transcends self-interest.

How does the commitment to cultivating unity play
out in what follows in Acts? The text is far too dense and
multifaceted to claim that this issue is explicitly prioritized,
but it does constitute a discernible subtext. Pervo identifies
the author as writing in Greek, probably in Ephesus about
115 CE, and having a strong familiarity with the Greek
version of the Hebrew Scriptures. This suggests a gentile
thoroughly immersed in Scripture with a cosmopolitan
outlook. He would also be an accomplished storyteller who
had learned many narrative techniques and could deploy
them with impressive skill.

He adopted anonymity because the name of an actual
human author would seriously compromise the technique
of narrative omniscience attached to sacred writings, for
such texts are presumed to be composed by, or rather dic-
tated to, someone inspired by God. (Thus it was that for
centuries illuminated manuscripts of the Bible often carried illustrations of the Holy Spirit in the form of a bird
perched somewhere near the writer's ear.) Irenaeus (c. 180
CE) makes a case for Luke as the author of Acts—or more
correctly, the implied author: he was evidently familiar

with Paul's letters and oral traditions about him, had access to copies of Josephus's works and to the sayings sources for the gospels of Matthew, Mark and Luke.[2]

At the time when Acts was written, a fundamental problem for the young Christian community was the validity of the mission to the gentiles: that is, the extension and cultivation of their "unity" beyond the original Jewish group gathered in Jerusalem. This community daily attended the temple, where Peter preached to the "Men of Israel" that "the God of Abraham, Isaac and Jacob, the God of our fathers, had glorified Jesus" (Acts 3:13). So when the author says that they devoted themselves to "cultivating unity," we know that they were already united as pious Jews. The challenge was to extend that unity.

This difficulty was decisively confronted in the longest narrative in Acts. Pervo entitles it *"Conversions of Peter and Cornelius"* (Acts 10:1–22). The plural form "conversions" marks the priority as well as the necessity of Peter's conversion. He both needed and underwent conversion to the prospect of cultivating a unity that could include a Roman centurion like Cornelius. Although "pious and God-fearing," the latter was presumably an uncircumcised non-Jew stationed in Caesarea, and obviously wealthy, with servants and a home large enough to accommodate his friends and relations. To this rather unlikely candidate appeared an angel, who ordered him to invite Simon, surnamed Peter, to his house. Summoning two servants and a soldier and having told them what had happened to him, he sent them to Joppa where Peter was lodging.

Meanwhile, Peter fell into a trance:

> He had a vision of an object like a large cloth suspended by its four corners that descended from the opened sky to the ground. In it were all the four-legged animals and reptiles of earth and all the birds of the sky. A voice said: "Go kill and eat these creatures." "Certainly not,

sir," he answered. "I have never tasted anything that was unclean and impure." The voice from above spoke again: "Stop designating 'unclean' what God has made pure." This was repeated twice more, after which the whole apparatus was hauled back up into the sky. (Acts 10:11–16)

As Pervo notes, "The voice contrasts Peter's views with those of God, who counts all clean" by alluding to Genesis 1:24–25 in which the Creator affirms the goodness of all creation.[3] As Peter was struggling to make sense of his vision, Cornelius's men arrived. The Spirit ordered Peter to go and make himself known to the men, who in reply told him that Cornelius had been directed by an angel of God to invite Peter to his house. The next day they set out together and, in anticipation of their arrival, Cornelius invited his relatives and close friends to join him. When Peter arrived, Cornelius fell on his knees in homage but Peter pulled him to his feet saying, "I too am mortal!"

As they entered the house, Peter told the gathering that although Jews were forbidden to associate intimately with or visit those of another race, *"God has shown me that no person is unclean or impure"* (Acts 10:28), and therefore he had come when summoned. He asked Cornelius to explain why he invited him. Cornelius told him about his vision and the resulting group of his relatives and friends now gathered in the sight of God to hear what the Lord has directed Peter to say.

Then Peter spoke:

"I am beginning to grasp," replied Peter, "that God really is non-discriminatory and accepts all who revere him and conduct themselves properly, regardless of national or ethnic background." (Acts 10:34–35)

Pervo characterizes this and the following verses as "Peter's single sermon to gentiles. . . . The first reported instance of the cultural adaptation of the Christian message to particular circumstances."4 The political "circumstances" are those represented by the Roman Empire in the person of Cornelius. The distinctive theme is that of a universalism based on "the universal God" rather than on Trajan's imperial rule. This God discriminates, if at all, only on the basis of conduct; not on the grounds of ethnicity or political power.

Peter's astonishing sermon is even more astonishing when read today. For contemporary Christianity is characterized by schisms, crusades, denominational infighting, and discrimination against other religions—in each case based on claims to a God-given right or even duty to discriminate. In direct contrast, the sermon is clearly the fruit of Peter's conversion to a God who, having created every living being clean and pure, is to be revered in turn by everyone regardless of national, ethnic or religious background. This is the basis on which Peter and the other apostles are to cultivate unity. The key message is that we cannot set any boundaries to this endeavor, because like all other beings we are part of an already existing, overarching unity based on our creation by God. This is true whether we ignore it or deny it, and whether we aim to cultivate it or claim to have achieved it according to our own standards and perceptions.

It is this truth that underlies the story of *both* conversions, that of Peter as well as that of Cornelius. Note, too, that Cornelius responds immediately and positively to what he is told to do in his vision, while Peter *argues* about his orders. He rather than Cornelius has to be converted to realizing their pre-existing unity. It meant he could no longer identify some people, as opposed to all others, as "worthy" to participate in his community's life and work; neither could he decree that only "Jewish" Christians could be identified as followers of Jesus. Nor that they alone are entitled to share in the physical and spiritual life support systems of the original apostolic community.

Most importantly, the narrative tells us that this clear challenge to an "apartheid" Christian identity comes directly *from God*. The first recorded conversion of a politically identified gentile after the death of Jesus is in no sense due to Peter's individual decision. Quite the contrary. It comes about through the Spirit's express command and in the face of sustained pious resistance on Peter's part. This supports the view that the fundamental problem for Jesus' Jewish followers was the validity of the gentile mission. More than anything else, this spiritual myopia of theirs exposes the gulf between divine intention and human understanding.[5]

Peter's religious rhetoric might be seen as preempting and reinforcing the intent of civil anti-discrimination laws today. Having said that, if we look at Christian communities, their religious norms are now routinely used to discriminate against others, including "other" Christians. Thus the case of Cornelius—who personifies political power—also dramatizes the secular non-discriminatory ideal underlying *koinonia*. Indeed, it is often his "pagan" judgment that insists on its implementation by religious authorities; for today all too many nominally Christian hearts and church tribunals betray Peter's acceptance of a nondiscriminatory God. Instead they exemplify human partiality in its most pious modes and manifestations, and thus stand in direct conflict with divine impartiality.

Moreover, this contrast is even more striking if we take Peter's vision of God as seriously as he did, and make it an overriding factor and motivation in our conduct toward all other beings. For the divine argument that enjoins nondiscrimination—by human against human—is based on the cleanliness, purity, and goodness of other-than-human creatures. The goodness of *their* creaturehood is guarantor of ours. If they are "good" by virtue of being created by God, then it follows that we are, too. Created before us, they are necessarily presupposed in setting the standard and grounds on which God displays impartiality to all beings—including us. This echoes Paul's throwaway remark in regard to the uncircumcised gentiles: "God shows no partiality" (Galatians 2:6).

Such a judgment of our status before God goes against all common valuations of ourselves in relation to other creatures. The paradox at the heart of Peter's conversion reverses all our preconceptions about ourselves in relation to all other species; about their and our relationship to God. We may no longer assume that if we show partiality toward some non-human creatures, then so too does God. In fact, it is the other way round. God's impartiality toward all creatures is established as the true basis for non-discrimination within the human community of life on Earth. The story of Peter's conversion is a parable disclosing the unpalatable truth that when we attribute partiality to God, we are in fact reducing God to an image of ourselves. Worse yet, instead of cultivating unity between ourselves, God, and all other beings, we destroy it—and do so in God's name!

ൟ

The original difficulty this story of Peter would have posed for its presumed audience, says Pervo, is that it compresses too much thought derived from different sources into a brief space.[6] It is no less difficult for us today. Overall it begs the question of how we compare with Peter in implementing the commands of a universal God. Do we who call ourselves Christian cultivate an image of God that fosters unity? Or, do we presume that God favors those who believe in Jesus as 'his Son' over those who do not? Or do we imagine that one gender, class, or race of mortals takes precedence over another? In regard to other species, do we use clever arguments like the "Anthropic Principle" to prove that God favors the human species over all others? Answering these questions about the kind of God we claim to believe in and what we believe about ourselves is as demanding of us as it was of Peter. Stressing the impartiality of God's love drives home the partiality of our own.

It shows up in the fact that while political commissions and legislatures seek to deal with entrenched prejudices by outlawing discrimination, Christianity seems irretrievably split between its Eastern and Western branches and their offshoots. In Jerusalem today, Christianity is officially represented by eleven denominations: Greek Orthodox, Armenian Orthodox, Syrian Orthodox, Latin Catholics, Greek Catholics (Melkites), Maronites, Chaldeans, Syrian Catholics, Armenian Catholics, Roman Catholics and Anglicans, all with patriarchal ecclesiastical courts ruling on family law—that is, on marriage, divorce, child custody, alimony, adoption, etc. It is hardly surprising that cultivating unity between Christians, Jews, and Muslims now appears to be primarily a political issue rather than a religious ideal or goal.

A closer look at God's ground-breaking lesson in impartiality increases the discomfort. Peter was rebuked for discriminating against other species on the grounds of their "uncleanness." He resisted the message just as strongly as we do, indeed so strongly that God had to repeat it three times. Finally, he got it: he understood that their "cleanness" was based not on our reactions to them but on their having been created, like ourselves, by God. As in the Prologue to John's Gospel, so also in the Acts narrative we discern a reference to the Genesis text and to our pre-existing unity. *All things* made by God are good simply by virtue of having been made by God. This resonates with the scientific argument for our pre-existing unity based on our common origins: on a shared genetic life-bond between us and all other species, on a fundamental mutual participation in life and in death. When Cornelius kneels before him Peter insists:

> I, too, am mortal! (*kai ego autos anthropos eimi*). (Acts 10:26)

Cornelius's prostration was a gesture of reverence for the divine he saw manifested in Peter and in his mission. This shows not only how the apostles were perceived but also that they had to resist such attributions of supernatural status.[7] To be mortal means to experience life on earth for an allotted span of time—a definitive distinction between human and divine existence. Despite the claims of cryogenicists, mortality remains the shared characteristic of all living beings, human and non-human alike. Peter's declaration echoes that of Pilate presenting Jesus to the people before his death and saying, "Behold, a mortal man!" (*idou ho anthropos!* John 19:5–4). Our mortality unites us, both as individuals and as a species, with all the living and the dead. It unites us with earth, the *ground* of our unity with all beings. There, both the reality and the image of cultivating unity find their basic form and truth.

When Peter and Cornelius met, coming as they did from very different backgrounds, their differences were profound and the adjustments required of them profounder still, for they represented two opposing conceptions of unity: the *koinon* or *council* of Roman imperial power in nearby Galatia and the *koinonia* of the Jerusalem community. *Koinon* was based on and expressed the ability of Rome to impose unity and order on other nations and people by force of arms. *Koinonia*, as we have seen, was inspired by a vision of a universal, non-discriminatory

God, creator of all beings. Both were powerful instruments for cultivating unity. The fundamental difference between them was that Rome used military force to impose its vision and sanctioned that action by invoking the divine power of Caesar. The direct antithesis of that was Peter's vision of creating unity based on the manifest creative power of a universal God.

Having attained the rank of centurion of the Italic Cohort, Cornelius was a privileged representative of imperial power. His name evokes one of the most distinguished and venerable of Roman patrician clans.[8] He would have been familiar with the concept of *koinon* and its practice in nearby Galatia. He is described as "pious and God-fearing," both terms attesting not only to his piety toward the God of Israel (Acts 10:2) but also his filial allegiance to Rome.[9] Piety (*pietas*) was a core Roman value that bound together members of the family, members of society, humankind, and the gods. It was at the same time religious and political, individual and collective, holding both society and family in balance. *Pietas* held the imperial Galatian *koinon* together by emphasizing the element of union in both community and commonwealth. A powerful tool used for this purpose was imperial religion, a praxis that included the building and maintenance of temples dedicated to Caesar and the goddess Roma, together with public celebrations involving processions, prayers, sacrifices, and games honoring Caesar and promoting the well-being of the Roman Empire.[10]

The profound differences in lifestyle, religion, and culture between this quintessential Roman, Cornelius, and Peter, a Jewish Galilean fisherman, could not be greater. They reflect the cultural mismatch that made the process of cultivating unity within the apostolic *koinonia* a continuing challenge. For they symbolize two opposing models of divine power: imperial *koinon* based on military power and union with Rome as against Christian *koinonia* based on peacemaking, community building, union with the crucified Jesus, and a particular concern for the poor.

෬෧

The latter qualities are borne out by Paul's understanding of this unity:

> God is faithful, by whom you were called into *koinonia* with his son, Jesus Christ. The cup of blessing that we bless, is it not *koinonia* in the blood of Christ? The bread that we break, is it not *koinonia* in the body of Christ? (1 Corinthians 1:9)

> For they gave according to their means, as I can testify, and beyond their means, of their own free will, begging us earnestly for the favor of practicing *koinonia* in the relief of the saints. (2 Corinthians 8:3–4)

> Under the test of this service (to the poor) you will glorify God by your obedience in acknowledging the gospel of Christ and your generosity in practising *koinonia* for them and for all others. (2 Corinthians 9:13)

> The grace of our Lord Jesus Christ, and the love of God and the *koinonia* of the Holy Spirit be with you all. (2 Corinthians 13:13)

In his letter to the Galatians, Paul describes how the problem of assimilating uncircumcised gentiles was resolved by the practice of *koinonia*. But assimilation was not only a Jewish problem; such a union would also present a stumbling-block for the imperial *koinon* of Galatia. Paul tells the Galatian *ekklesias* or communities that when he went to Jerusalem for the second time he took with him the uncircumcised Titus. He notes that the brethren there did not compel him to be circumcised, even though he was a Greek. On the contrary, he reported, their meeting developed into a ritual of peacemaking and a practice of solidarity in which they extended "the right hand of community" (*dexias koinōnias*) to Paul and Titus.[11]

> And when they perceived the grace that was given to me, James and Cephas and John, reputed to be pillars, gave the right hand of *koinonia* to me and Barnabas, that we should go to the gentiles and they to the circumcised; only they would have us remember the poor, which I was eager to do. (Galatians 2:9–10)

However, Brigitte Kahl notes, from the perspective of Rome *koinonia* between messianic Jews and uncircumcised Gauls or Galatians must have appeared as an upsetting irregularity. It implied lawless conduct and disturbed the *koinon* inasmuch as it interfered with provincial reverence for the divine emperor and failed to comply with the principles of the imperial cosmos. Uncircumcised Galatians who accepted both circumcised Jews as their brothers and the Jewish God as their common father constituted an identity, a community, and a model of worship that was not only ambiguous in terms of Jewish law, but worse yet was illicit in its civic consequences within the framework of Roman law.

On a symbolic level, it looked like another blasphemous Gallic-barbarian attack on the core principles of Roman rule and order that laid down the *appropriate* form of association between Galatians and Jews. This Pauline community offered a unity and an affiliation beyond the power of Caesar to define or control; more dangerous still, it was defined by and subject to the authority of a crucified rebel leader in Roman Judea. It offered a "universalism from below" that was totally incompatible with the principles of imperial "universalism from above," for "the divine Caesar alone was entitled to set the terms and conditions for licit interaction between Jews and Galatians, not his crucified antagonist."[12]

This archetypal conflict between contrasting visions of unity based on divinity, between imperial divine power and the unifying, universal love of God, has been part of the history of Christianity since Constantine's conversion. With that conversion, membership in the *koinon* became Christianity's prerequisite. Imperial power, centered in Constantinople, Rome, and their surrogate jurisdictions, set the terms and conditions for a "universalism from above." But its continuing critique has been "a universalism from below"—the recovery of a *koinonia* exemplified in the life and death of the crucified (rebel) leader, Jesus, and inspired by his teaching and dedication to nonviolence.

> If there is any encouragement in Christ, any incentive to love, any *koinonia* in the Spirit, any affection and sympathy, complete my joy by being of the same mind, having the same love, being in full accord and of one mind. (Philippians 2:1–2)

For Paul, the term *koinonia* expresses the bond between Jesus and God; between Father, Son, and Spirit; between Christians and Jesus; Christian and Christian; Christian and non-Christian; Christians and the poor. Jesus' understanding of *koinonia* emerges in his use of parable, where it challenges myths of imperial power and their "universalism from above." Several aspects of these challenges will be discussed in the following chapter. We then go on to discern the subversive character of parable—and with it, Jesus' universalism "from below."

2

MYTH AND PARABLE

> We are accustomed to think of myths as the
> opposite of science. But in fact they are a central
> part of it: the part that decides its significance in
> our lives. So we very much need to understand
> them. Myths are not lies. Nor are they detached
> stories. They are imaginative patterns, networks of
> powerful symbols that suggest particular ways of
> interpreting the world. They shape its meaning.
> —Mary Midgley, *The Myths We Live By*, p. 1

In order to understand the narrative form known as parable, something must first be said about myth, the longer narrative form that is both antecedent to parable and from which the latter derives its peculiar force. What follows here is necessarily a summary, for the word "myth" is ambiguous: it can be and is used in two quite different ways. Sometimes, it is applied to a sacred story in which the protagonist or hero is in every way superior to us. This is exemplified in Homer's *Odyssey*, which begins *in medias res* and then moves backward to accommodate the present situation of the story-teller; in short it is a literary narrative rather than an historical account. Alternatively, as with the Aristotelian *mythos*, or plotted tale, the term may indicate a creative way of integrating a variety of incidents into one complete and dynamic story. In either case "myth" designates a chosen modality for interpreting the world in a particular way.

Adopting the Aristotelian model gives us a Bible that reflects a grand and in some degree predetermined plot of world history, with each subordinate literary plot a sort of miniature version of the overarching plan that joins Genesis and Apocalypse. It ties a beginning to an ending, and proposes to the imagination the triumph of concord over discord.[1] The peculiar power of parable derives directly from its ability to challenge this mythic triumph and so tease us into further thought.

But analysis of form is not the only possible approach, for Roland Barthes defines myth linguistically as a type of speech, a system of communication, a message or mode of signification.[2] This focus on signification presupposes and emphasizes that myths communicate their messages through images, symbols, and stories that both suggest and reflect particular ways of interpreting the world. In preliterate societies they functioned as cosmic paradigms, as creation narratives that were recited and ritually re-enacted. A society's traditions were encoded in such myths and their shared ownership helped constitute its group identity.[3] These ritualized interpretations of an oral culture's beliefs gave narrative form to communal or individual experience and thus mediated reality for the group in ways that literate cultures can achieve only by conscious effort and even then without general consent.

Yet we tend to think of early oral cultures as simply illiterate or preliterate, defining them in terms of things that we have and they do not. But thinking of them in terms of their relationship to writing is the equivalent, says Walter Ong, of working out the biology of a horse in terms of what goes on in an automobile factory. Whereas the letters of the alphabet are seen to have their existence in space, speech as sound creates no similarly discernible effects. Yet we must respect the fact that sound implies movement and thus implies change. This means that the oral-aural world, even more than the world of our other senses, immediately involves and affects our mental processes. These processes, particularly those associated with the imagination, are not only set in motion but acted upon by spoken words. Moreover, this intellectual activity is related to what is heard in ways that differ sharply from our visual or tactile activities. The world of written words is quite different from the sound world.[4]

This active oral-aural element in myths dealing with the beginning or creation of the world was the basis for their ritual enactment in various forms, times, and places. In contemporary western cultures, a blurred reflection of this can be seen in the annual marking of different seasons: religiously in church services, and commercially in shop windows and greeting cards. Ricoeur sums up the conjunction of word and action thus: "What the myth says, the ritual performs." Through such performances successive generations experience a "participatory belonging" that provides historical continuity to a society and, as generation succeeds generation, defines its members.[5]

In his seminal study of this phenomenon, *Cosmos and History: The Myth of the Eternal Return*, Mircea Eliade notes many important differences between preliterate societies and modern ones. Two are particularly pertinent here. First, every member of an archaic society felt indissolubly connected with the Cosmos—the world-order that emerged from chaos at the moment of creation—and with cosmic seasonal and natural rhythms. This encouraged a sense of "participatory belonging" that in most societies is now ritualized only by religious communities. Today our strongest individual connections and most important self-identification are not with the Cosmos but with recorded human history. In archaic societies, however, the Cosmos

too had a history, a "sacred history" preserved and transmitted through myths. This is echoed in the phrase "when
all things began" in John 1:1 and Genesis 1:1. And it was
this sacred cosmic history that also preserved and transmitted the social paradigms and exemplary models for all the
activities engaged in by members of those societies.

Secondly and more pertinently, the metaphysical concepts of the ancient world were not formulated in theoreti-
cal language but expressed poetically in symbols, in recita-
tion, and in ritual enactment of myths. This is made clear
in a new translation of John's Gospel where the prologue
is laid out in the form of Semitic poetry (Miller, *Complete
Gospels*, pp. 209–10) and employs appropriate discursive
and syntactic features of language to facilitate the emergence of a complex system of coherent affirmations about
ultimate reality. It is useless, Eliade says, to search archaic
languages for the terms so laboriously created by the great
western philosophical traditions. Such words as "being,"
"nonbeing," "real," "unreal," "becoming," and "illusory"
are not found in the language of the Australian aborigines
or among those of the ancient Mesopotamians:

> But if the word is lacking, the thing is present; only
> it is "said"—that is, revealed in a coherent fashion—
> through symbols and myths.[6]

For all these reasons, outside the field of literary, an-
thropological or religious studies—and whether in the
context of saga, tale, or straightforward narrative—the
term "myth" is now commonly used and understood in
the derogatory sense of being false and misleading. Indeed
even within those fields some have offered trenchant
criticisms of myth that have negatively affected scholarly
investigation. Emile Durkheim quotes Max Müller's radical
distinction between mythology and religion, reserving the
name of religion only for those beliefs that "conform to the

prescriptions of a sane moral system and a rational theology." For him, myths were parasitic growths that attached themselves to these fundamental concepts and denatured them.[7]

Durkheim dismisses Müller's distinction as arbitrary, observing with Ricoeur that if myth were withdrawn from religion, it would be necessary to deny the importance of rites also. Nevertheless, the unwarranted distinction between myth on the one hand and truth or rationality on the other has persisted—and has served to discount and marginalize the importance of myth. Part of the reason for this is a persistent claim that myths belong to the past, to an archaic and indeed pre-rational era in human history that was dominated by imagination rather than recorded facts and motivated by cult and emotion rather than sophisticated concepts and the dissemination of ideas. Moreover, it has been argued that the collective ethos of ancient societies was not congenial to individual initiative or the accumulation of wealth, both of which are seen as essential in "healthy capitalist" societies.

But as Mary Midgley points out, myths are not lies or false statements to be contrasted with truth, reality, fact, or history. In its positive and enduring sense, says Wendy Doniger, myth is a story that is sacred to and shared by a group of people who find their most important meanings in it; although composed in the past about events in the past, it continues to have meaning in the present. Plato deconstructed the myths of Homer and Hesiod, but recognizing that people require myths, he constructed new ones for them.

> He transformed ancient mythic themes to make the myth of Eros and the myth of the creation of the universe (Timaeus), and he actually applied the word myth (which he called *muthos,* since he spoke ancient Greek)

to the story of the world that he created in the Phaedo
and to the myth of Er that he created at the end of the
Republic.[8]

Doniger comments that Plato dismissed as lies any myths
he disapproved of (that is, those created by nurses and
poets and other such people), but accepted the myths that
he liked (such as those he created himself) as truths. This
ambivalence in the definition of myth endures, she says, to
the present day. The problem was laid bare when, on the
advice of Nobel laureate William Golding, James Lovelock
gave the name "Gaia" to his scientific theory of the evolution of life on Earth. It was originally the name of the
primal Earth deity in Hesiod's *Theogony*, which tells of the
birth of the gods and the development of the cosmic order.
This mythic genealogy of a generation of gods is followed
by myths that narrate that generation's future history.[9]

As Lovelock later wrote, its mere association with myth
and story-telling led people to assume that his theory was
"bad science." As a result, it was almost impossible for a
scientist to publish a paper on Lovelock's theory that did
not disparage it. Metaphorical phrases such as "Gaia likes
it cool," intended to express the observation that the Earth
system appears to have flourished in glacial times, had to
be discarded. One could speak, Lovelock said, only in the
strict language of science, laden with abstract nouns and
the passive voice. The definitive rebuttal was that the Gaia
theory seemed like a religious belief—empirically untest-
able, and therefore in its present day context incapable of
further rationalization.

Still, he held firmly to the title, not least because en-
vironmentalists and others pointed out to him that Gaia
was too important a focus for thought and action to be
conscripted or restricted by science alone. Now, over thirty
years later, scientific insights based on Gaia theory are routinely discussed worldwide and accepted by those with and

without scientific training. As Lovelock says, ancient belief and modern knowledge fused emotionally in the awe with which astronauts saw the Earth revealed in all its shining beauty against the deep darkness of space.

This image and its effects on our imagination do not prove that Earth lives. But the idea that it resembles a superorganism, able to regulate its climate and composition so as always to be comfortable for the living organisms that inhabit it, has enlarged the public vision and created a global context within which regional climatic variations can be viewed and better understood. However, even as Gaia theory is now educating us about Ricoeur's notion of "participatory belonging" and Eliade's image of being "indissolubly connected with the Cosmos," scientists remain reluctant to deal in such symbols and metaphors. Their work is focused on experiments aimed at particular applications. As a result, insights derived from Gaia theory tend to find acceptance primarily at a subliminal level—thanks largely to modern media that graphically present geographical, climatic, ecological, and geophysical scientific data in ways accessible to all.

So the discovery of long and short term interactions linking the evolution of the Greenland Ice Cap, industries in Detroit, and deforestation in New Guinea has led to a better understanding of the many and diverse factors that contribute to what is called global climate change. Now, too, the impact of our communal and individual relationships on all such factors is routinely calculated under the heading of "carbon capture;" and governments worldwide try to take account of these interconnections in their future policies, knowing that they are understood and assimilated at levels other than the purely rational.[10]

But the contemptuous rejection of Lovelock's theory on the grounds that it is "like a religious belief" demonstrates contemporary difficulties in understanding myths as cultural phenomena. The reason, of course, is that non-empirical modes of thought go against a culture in which individualism has overcome a natural sense of participatory belonging and thus deafens us to appeals that we diminish our consumption of resources. Within that horizontal world, allegedly the only one, mythic truth must be identified, dissected, and reappropriated in "rational" form. The myth must be cloaked in graphs, computer models and algorithms, displayed as facts, data, or static nuggets of information abstracted from the lived situations in which they arise and through which they continue to influence our lives. Yet there is hope, for at the very same time information in the form of such symbols as "our ecological footprint" is being readily incorporated into our lived experience, echoing and resonating with our own conscious encounters and bodily connectedness with the environment.

Mary Midgley warns us against three current idols of the marketplace: the social-contract myth, the progress myth and the myth of omnicompetent science. The three are connected, she says, not only in that they need rethinking, but because the third impedes our efforts to deal with the first two. The danger is that all three myths tend to exalt form over substance, method over aim, and precision of detail over comprehensiveness of scope. Agreeing with her, I would add a further element. All three emerge from and are focused on human history and our place in it rather than on cosmic history, a scientific discipline we now understand as the evolution of planetary life support systems and the dependence of all species—including our own—upon them.

This last conceptual complex—what Midgley calls "the claims of nature"—together with our common interest in honoring them, has proved surprisingly difficult for those of our cultural heritage to grasp. While this is due in no small part to the fact that the environmental alarm is much more recent than the social one, it is also more difficult to incorporate such claims into the framework of a contract that we can sign and expect to profit from. "No one has yet made coral reefs or Siberian tundra our fellow citizens," she pointedly observes. Yet even in the short term, and certainly in the longer, the claims and interests of nature will, as she says, be seen to converge with ours.[11]

In this situation, myths and parables that apparently transcend human interest or interests can still be eloquent if we wake up to the imaginative power that shaped them. There seems to be a deep impulse in human nature to orient itself in and toward the unknown by pictorial representations, imaginative dramatizations and narratives. The metaphor, the fable, the myth, and the parable (the last three being in fact extended metaphors) represent a kind of preliminary science. They are pre-liminal in that they bring us to the threshold of what is now called science. But they are more than science, since in them intellect is only part of knowing.

This means that we should not allow the often obsolete elements of older myths and epics to obscure their essential vision. Indeed, those negative cultural reactions to myth noted by Durkheim and evident in reactions to Gaia theory can also be found within religious communities and within biblical scholarship. Amos Wilder sees there a comparable reaction rooted in an anxiety that the Christian gospel should be extricated from its mythological legacies. In this empirical age of ours, he remarks, we are told that "the theologian as well as the preacher should confine himself [sic] to a secular idiom." Therefore, we should turn from the supernatural and apocalyptic imaginings of the apostles to the earthly aphorisms and comparisons of Jesus— and especially to the *nonmythological* parables. For this characteristic form of his teaching is secular through and through and therefore, so the argument goes, is as eloquent and negotiable in the twentieth century as in the first.[12]

This desire to separate myth from the Christian gospel gave birth in the twentieth century to the "de-mythologizing" of the New Testament, a term originating in the work of Rudolf Bultmann. The German *Entmythologisierung* refers to what he saw as the necessity of recovering the present, existential demand of the biblical Pauline message of the *kerygma*, the proclamation of redemption, from the "outmoded" worldview implicit in the vocabulary and assumptions of the biblical writers. This demythologizing meant learning to think without images, that is, relating the religious tradition to contemporary events in one's life.

After 1945, notably in the context of the horrors of the Holocaust, this meant breaking through the long-standing separation between biblical and contemporary realities. It became a major endeavor to show that religious parables are still relevant after Auschwitz; that in Jesus' stories we have "parables for our time"—whatever they may have meant in his.[13] But this whole approach to Jesus' teaching too readily overlooked the wider symbolic or mythic elements that he both inherited and adapted to his purposes. For his parables acquire their peculiar logic by virtue of being narratives within a narrative, situated within the all-encompassing narrative of the deliverance by God of the covenanted people, Israel.

In that "Ur-myth," a narrative that ranges over the sacred history of an entire people,[14] the gospels find their basic presuppositions and larger context. Many of Jesus' parables, even within the spheres of life that framed them, would have been simply ambiguous except for their orientation to a prior mythical horizon that was summed up in the phrase, "the kingdom of God." This formula in considerable measure epitomized the basic religious orientation of those who heard him. If it now sounds anachronistic, that is because it grew out of a first-century religious world-view that now has few adherents.

A cosmic paradigm of Yahweh's kingship is presented throughout the biblical record, together with a prophetic critique of its abuse by successive kings of Israel. There are passages that stress the range and timelessness of Yahweh's sovereignty over past and future alike (Exodus 15:18; 1 Samuel 12:12; Psalm 145:11f; 146:10). Pre-exilic writings describe Yahweh as Israel's King and promise help, deliverance, justice and joy for the chosen people. The exilic and post-exilic writings also abound in pointers to Yahweh's kingship over the world.[15] Some such larger time-representation and world-representation provided the proper context for a biblical faith based on the creation narratives of Genesis and their later interpretation in books such as Job.

It is important to note that within this mythic continuum the prophetic books offer a continuing critique of earthly kingship and human royal consciousness. When compared with the rule of Yahweh, that of the earthly monarch is often condemned as simply an agent of greater exploitation by the powerful.[16] Without this backcloth of a wider vision of kingship, the further critique of exploitative power systems embedded in Jesus' parables and personified by him offers us only a diminished perspective.[17] We fail to see how the mythic *koinon* of the Roman Empire was subverted by his practice of *koinonia* and his death as "King of the Jews."

An important question thus arises: If parable is a form of narrative that has what Ricoeur calls "the power of disclosure" and the ability to redescribe reality, what kind of reality is at stake? Is it, as the demythologizers would have it, solely the reality of our existence here and now? Or are Jesus' parables addressed only to the reality of a first-century Jew? In the latter case they remain stories that take to its historical limits the continuum of the Jewish

tradition of the kingdom of God in ordinary and established language. But, demythologizers may reasonably
point out, the reality of first-century Judaism is not our
reality today. Nor can their worldview be ours, especially
since for the first time in human history we have seen our
entire world, planet Earth, from a point outside it.

Is there, then, no continuity between first-century
understanding and ours? Tania Oldenhage finds one in
Ricoeur's proposal that parables "transgress" traditional
forms of language by means of intensification of or bring-
ing-to-the-limit an already constituted language. They are
poetic discourse insofar as they have the power to disclose
a special referent through their outlandish, excessive, and
eccentric traits. They take traditional religious language to
its limits and stir the imagination to find new meaning in
it. The sayings of Jesus are thus to be understood as "limit-
expressions" under pressure of which traditional forms of
discourse have been shattered.[18]

And continue to be shattered. How does this happen?
How do Jesus' parables take language about the kingdom of
God to its limits and beyond them into our contemporary
world? The short answer from Ricoeur is "intertextuality":
the way in which the metaphor "the kingdom of God" is
transferable between texts within the Bible that have been
and are read at different moments in history.[19] This the-
matic metaphor emerges naturally from the Jewish texts
that Jesus knew and so aptly used. Every time he related the
kingdom of heaven to events involving a human agent—
"The kingdom of heaven is . . . like a woman who . . ."
(Matthew 13:33)—his audience captured simultaneously
his particular and his universal view of that kingdom.

In reading Jesus' parables today, the intertextuality of
the Bible provides us with this diachronic alternation and
contrast—and not only between the Jewish "landscape" up

to the time of Jesus and the view he had of it during his life under the Roman Empire. For the force diagrams have modern vectors as well. The "fool" in his parable of the rich farmer (Luke 12:16–20) bears a marked resemblance to the bankers and traders responsible for the present financial crisis. Being able to include that "up-close-and-personal" view, we can grasp the clash between the farmer's situation and that of his hearers—and also that between Jesus' view of reality and that of his audience. Our view includes that telescopic one as well as the microscopic one we receive in the text. And both of these are available to us despite the nearsighted view we have of our own personal, historical, and global contexts.

Laid out programmatically, this seems a long and rather tortuous process of assimilation. In fact, the clash of views that results from these different perspectives can and does occur almost simultaneously: especially if we *hear* the parable rather than read it.[20] John Dominic Crossan, using an image from Rilke, describes this moment as "the dark interval":

> I am the pause between two notes that fall
> Into a real accordance scarce at all:
> Both, though, are reconciled in the dark interval,
> tremblingly.

This internalizing, this thought-induced trembling, is the product of an imaginative response to the power that parables have to reorient our views and change our perspective. Parables, says Crossan, are supposed to overturn one's structure of expectation; and therein and thereby they threaten the security of one's mythic, man-made world. The book of Jonah, as we shall see, is a parable not only against the entire prophetic tradition but against the very heart of the Bible itself. But, note well, it is against the Bible *within* the Bible. This made it a *story-event* for those Jews who heard it. And as they did so, something happened to their worldview: the particular parable subverted the overarching one created in and by myth.[21]

In Jesus' time this mythic framework incorporated what Eliade calls the ancient Hebrew cosmogonic-heroic myth, which implied the extinction by a King-Messiah of gentile kings including Pompey and Nebuchadnezzar.[22] The mythicization of historical personages reminds us that not only do parables present narratives within a narrative, but that for Christians they are narratives recounted by Jesus, the principal historic character in an all-encompassing narrative. And that narrative in turn derives its power of disclosure by contradicting the commonly shared perspective of an all-encompassing myth of divine or human kingship. This "similarity-in-difference" to contemporary myths of a "providentially" directed world order gives Jesus' parables their continuing imaginative force.

3

THE WORD TODAY

Myth establishes world. Apologue defends world.
Action investigates world. Satire attacks world.
Parable subverts world. It is clear, I hope, that
parable can only subvert the world created in and
by myth. There is no other world it can touch. It
is possible to live in myth and without parable.
But it is not possible to live in parable alone. To
live in parable means to dwell in the tension of
myth and parable.
—John Dominic Crossan, *The Dark Interval*,
   pp. 59–60

How do parables work? The short answer is by making us
hold two directly contrary pictures of reality *at the same
time*: the overarching one created by myth and the myth-
subverting one created by parable. In Jesus' parable of the
Pharisee and the toll collector, two men are praying in the
temple. The Pharisee thanks God for the fact that he is not
like the toll collector, that is, thieving, unjust, adulterous.
The toll collector does not even dare to raise his head, but
strikes his chest and prays to God for mercy. The temple
setting reinforces the religious stereotype that people's ac-
ceptability to God reflects their status in society.

Then comes the punch-line, directly reversing our expectations:

Let me tell you, the second man went back home vindi-
cated but the first did not. (Luke 18:14a, SV)

Jesus' verdict upset the conventional moral standard of the
time by placing someone qualified to interpret the Law

and proud of his self-proclaimed observance of it *below* one who openly acknowledged failure on both counts. That paradoxical judgment stunned those who heard it, for suddenly their mythic image of a beautiful home (the Law in the temple) was seen poised over an earthquake zone (God's judgment).

Today, wrote Robert Funk, such parabolic juxtaposition and consequent reversal of religious expectations occurs whenever we find ourselves and our attitudes toward others judged by the text:

> To use the pejorative analogy of the New Testament, the Pharisee is the one who insists that he is the interpreter of the text, whereas the sinner allows himself to be interpreted by the text.[1]

The fact that this left Funk himself playing the Pharisee's part would not have escaped him. With Crossan and others he explored the role of parable with all the available tools of linguistic scholarship. These act, he said, as a third party between us, both antecedent to and part of any and every conversation about parables that helps us understand them. He pursued this understanding because he feared that the theological function of parables could become "ghettoized," that is, appropriated by a religious Pharisaical caste with the result that the words used become a barrier to understanding rather than a way through to it.[2]

This can happen because the language in which Jesus was later proclaimed as Lord was itself historically determined. From the fourth century on, concepts such as *preexistence, incarnation, resurrection, exaltation,* and *ascension* were used to talk about Jesus. Rapid changes in Christian settings—from Palestine to the Diaspora, from Jew to Gentile, from the context of imminent expectation to that of a deferred parousia, and from Jewish sect to a world religion—necessitated a corresponding series of reimaginings and translations.[3] In this situation, especially if removed from its context of mythic biblical narrative, an abstract category like "parable" offers us no way of connecting Jesus' teaching about the kingdom of God with living in the *koinon* of the Roman Empire; no way of understanding his teaching in the context of his fellowship with those "from below" whom his religious and social culture considered sinners or outcasts. The inclusion of that context is fundamental to the practice as well as the success or failure of *koinonia*, that is, of cultivating unity. Stripped of their original religious and socio-cultural setting, Jesus' parables simply cannot be employed in ways that challenge and reshape the religious imagination of our time as they did in his. The sum of these considerations constitutes the long answer to how parable "works."

Another factor is also at play here. Interpreting the parable of the Pharisee and the toll collector not only invites, but indeed demands our paying attention to the contrasting images of the two characters, whether or not they are historically accurate. Amos Wilder was wise in recognizing imagination as a necessary component of all profound knowing and celebration; all remembering, realizing, and anticipating; all faith, hope and love:

> When imagination fails doctrines become ossified, witness and proclamation wooden, doxologies and litanies empty, consolations hollow and ethics legalistic. It is at the level of imagination that any full engagement with life takes place. Though theology strictly understood is an intellectual if not a discursive activity yet the work of the greatest theologians has always been shot through with the imagination.[4]

This is certainly true of the parables attributed to Jesus. He who was called "The Word" could not address us "without taking account of how language works."[5] Parable operates and is responded to at different imaginative levels in new and changing contexts. Its eventful character gives it a particularly resonant effect within our lived experience. This effect might now be described as a deconstruction of that experience:

> In a deconstruction, our lives, our beliefs and our practices are not destroyed but forced to reform and refigure—which is a risky business. In the New Testament this is called *metanoia*, or undergoing a fundamental change of heart.[6]

Through such deconstruction, transformation, or change, our creative participation in parable becomes an active grappling with the text, an interaction that calls for— though it may not lead immediately or even ultimately to—appropriate action. As we shall see in the case of Jonah, he represents a refusal to change. Each parabolic text offers an opportunity and stimulus for undergoing, accepting, or rejecting a change of heart. The Torah, say the rabbis, remains alive because the readers of each generation add their own contribution to the story.[7]

Contemporary responses to Jesus' eventful life and words are partly formed by and mixed with previous and present historic responses and by their necessary engagement with the "common sense" nature of language today. Clearly, this broadens the scope of responses beyond those coming from academic disciplines whose practitioners are dedicated to retranslating and reinterpreting texts in the light of new insights into their origins and whose work is done on behalf of the wider Christian community. Paradigmatic cases are Jerome's translation of the Greek Bible into the Latin Vulgate, Luther's translation of the Vulgate into the vernacular German of his day, and the King James or Authorized Version that was an English translation of the original Hebrew and Greek texts. Spread throughout and beyond the British Empire, it became the foundational text and template for later English versions.

An important milestone in this development was the invention of printing. From Luther's time onwards it was possible for lay people to have direct access to the Scriptures by means of a personal copy. Up to then, they could only hear it read and interpreted by ecclesiastics; now they could read the texts by themselves and to each other in their homes. This *Tischreden* (reading at one's own table) led to a vernacular theology that resonated perfectly with Jesus' use of parable. This development had and continues to have historic consequences for Christian communities throughout the world. These range all the way from *upholding* imperialism with its attendant violence to *challenging* the imperial power structures that oppress the poor. Walter Wink has become a highly respected spokesman for this challenge in such books as *Naming the Powers: Language and Power in the New Testament*; *Jesus and Nonviolence: A Third Way*; *Engaging the Powers: Discernment and Resistance in a World of Domination*; and *When the Powers Fall: Reconciliation in the Healing of Nations*.

The paradoxical coexistence of a "universalism from above" and a "universalism from below" in responses to reading the Bible does more than simply re-present the archetypal conflict between the *koinon* of imperial divine power and the *koinonia* of union within the all-embracing love of God. It also reminds us that the very nature of parable is to subvert the world created in and by myth—and that this is done in response to that world. To live in parable means to dwell in the tension of myth *and* parable. One can change one's allegiance from a particular myth (for example, capitalism) to another (for example, communism). For every myth can have an antimyth:

> But a parable is not an antimyth. It is a story deliberately calculated to show the limitations of myth. . . . It does not, as parable, replace one myth with another.[8]

This is the case, says Crossan, because myth is an agent of stability whereas parable is an agent of change. Therefore parable generates an unsettling experience, and our immediate reaction to it will be self-contradictory: "I don't know what you mean by that story but I'm certain I don't like it."[9] Jesus' parable of the Pharisee and the toll-collector did not suggest that, if offered the choice, Pharisees would opt to become toll-collectors or *vice versa*. Nor did Jesus' hearers expect this to happen. The current myth of social mobility raises such an expectation only to contradict it. For it conceals the fact that few individuals are able to change—let alone select—their position in society. Nor may we assume that they would want to. *But*, the parable says, this does not mean that God judges them the way society does—or the way they judge each other. Or, for that matter, the way they judge themselves.

This means that the social context of theological language and its promise of stability affect what Funk called its destiny. Parabolic language does not exist in isolation, because it is not a light that shines upon God; rather it is a light that shines *from* God, illuminating our existence. It is a gift that creates new possibilities of addressing and understanding the reality that approaches us. So language becomes a source of light that can again and again lighten up the darkness of existence.[10]

ᏻᏉ

The contemporary context illuminated by this gift is one where, for the first time in human history (consciously or not), we are concerned with describing, measuring, and quantifying the (in)visible impact of global climate change on ourselves and on other species with whom we share our earthly environment. The light that shines from many of Jesus' parables rightly illuminates the attendant darkness of existence for the poor, for indigenous peoples and for those species most adversely affected by the relentless pace at which, seduced by the myth of perpetual growth, rainforests are turned into pulp and marine ecosystems into fishmeal. All other species are united in their helplessness, powerless to do anything about their environments being reduced to subsidiary elements of a human economic system. Pythes is back in charge, but without his wife.

In this situation, the poor are both outsiders and victims in a culture of consumerism in all its aspects, such that the natural world is represented by columns of figures and those below the poverty line have no input into decisions that literally mean life and death to them. The smaller historic world of Jesus appears almost idyllic by comparison. Yet like his life and lifestyle, his parables and responses to the poor show that the oppression of the many by the few and of the powerless by the powerful was the focus of his universal concern. As it was then, so is it now.

Like the prophets before him, Jesus called for justice for "the widow, the orphan and the stranger in the land." His friendships with outcasts like toll-collectors, harlots, and sinners scandalized his contemporaries. By sharing their lives, their hunger, and their powerlessness, he became and was seen to be one of them. His consumption of Earth's resources depended on what was available, or not, in the communities in which he lived. Contrary to the canons of his own community he asked a despised outsider, a Samaritan woman, for water to quench his thirst. He defended his disciples when, hungry, they plucked heads of wheat on the Sabbath. His political powerlessness was definitively demonstrated by the manner of his death at the hands of Jewish and Roman authorities.

The Jesus of *The Sayings Gospel Q* trusted that like a human father, God would not substitute an inedible stone for a petitioner's daily loaf. But in a further stage of the Q trajectory, Jesus becomes the role model for those who do not test God by expecting stones to become loaves. The painful human awareness that one needs to be able to count on God for bread rather than a rock is overridden by the religious concern not to permit a diminished trust to question God's goodness. The issue is no longer food, but trust.[11]

———But for the victims of climate change today, the issue is still food; and their consumption is limited not only by the seasonal rotation of crops and the success or failure of the harvest but also by the unacknowledged *koinonia* of the wider relationship between us, the earth, and its other-than-human creatures. The prophets before Jesus knew this was intrinsic to the well-being of the land and its produce. The cultivating of unity was located in and connected inextricably to the character of our relationship with earth and its other-than-human inhabitants as well as with other people and with God. Hosea stated unequivocally that when there is no faithfulness, kindness, or knowledge of God in the land; when people break all moral bounds as murder follows murder and swearing, killing, lying, stealing, and adultery abound; then the land mourns and all who dwell in it grow feeble—not only the beasts of the field and the birds of the air, but even the fish, who are swept from the sea (Hosea 4:1–3).

When Hosea spoke, there was no evidence for this interaction between knowledge of God, the character of human relationships, and their effect on the health of the land and its inhabitants. Yet as Wilder notes, in the Scriptures "the word is married to actuality and has leverage on the real."[12] Contemporary ecological research supports the linkage and the leverage. For "out there in Nature" there is no such thing as a "final form." We are all participants in creating a global future that we can scarcely imagine, a yet-to-be world based on all kinds of interactions between us and other living beings. This was equally true of Hosea's murderous people, although he couched his analysis in terms of the quality of their relationships with each other and with God.

The quantifiable analyses of the causes of global warming presently available from scientists don't keep account of these qualitative kinds of relationship. And the feedback loop that connects religious and secular communities of knowledge does not always work positively on behalf of our relationships with other species. Fundamentalist Christians see climate change and its destructive effects on Earth and on members of all species (other than themselves) as part of a divine apocalyptic scenario culminating in the second coming of Christ. Therefore they regard attempts to preserve the global ecosystem as ungodly—because they serve to delay that event. This is borne out by Ray Hart's description of the toxic/healthy mix of our biblical interpretations as "the general muck-up in which contemporary theology participates."[13]

His image suits the present situation because of its inherently "earthy" character. Theological language necessarily includes healthy and unhealthy matter and forms. Some of the healthy modalities, like parable, could with careful cultivation nourish not only new theological life-forms, but ultimately all living beings. Even more relevant is Hart's comment that, thanks to the influence of the media, the muck-up "extends well beyond the individual and the groves of academe to the public at large."[14] Sanctioned by the often faint resonance of theological authority, this "muck-heap" of previously cherished notions about ourselves and our place in the world still has the potential for creating ideas and symbols that could be fruitful and life-enhancing. It is equally clear, of course, that some apocalyptic notions have borne highly toxic fruit. One thinks, for example, of James Jones' People's Temple, which organized a mass suicide in Jonestown, Guyana in November, 1978.

Speaking more generally, one must acknowledge the deeply entrenched religious notion that we possess power over all other creatures on the basis of our having a soul "like to God," and that it is possible to justify their destruction on the basis of saving that soul for a life beyond this one. While such religious concepts and language no longer have direct support in civil society, they continue to influence the public domain through legal entitlements to ownership and use of land, the products of that land, and the species dependent thereon. To that degree Hart is right when he says that dogma is severed from its roots in religious imagination and becomes merely "a counter in an intricate intellectual chess game or a piece of outright ideology." Religiously, such images exert on our will no immediate pressure for change, for they fail to configure our experience and present knowledge of human life and of Nature.[15]

Against this trend, I intend to delve into this muck-heap by using some of its major texts, dominant symbols, and new translations to find what, if anything, lies within them that can help cultivate an understanding of our pre-existing unity and thereby nourish religious imagination today. To give an example: like many Christians, I grew up with the petitions of the Lord's Prayer helping to establish the nature of my relationship with God. In particular, "Lead us not into temptation" signaled that I depended on God to shield me from devilish attacks on my virtue, with those attacks embodied in evil people, places, and activities. Then I came across an alternative translation of the Greek version of this petition in *The Sayings Gospel Q*. It reads, "Do not put us to the test!"[16]

For me, at any rate, this transformed the meaning of the prayer from one that led me to expect an all-powerful God to shield me from "occasions of sin" to one that indicated I might expect to be tested by them. The onus is on me, not on God. This strikes a more authentic chord in a post-Enlightenment culture that values personal autonomy and places directly at my doorstep any responsibility for willfully contributing to harmful climate change. At its most basic, translation requires more than finding an equivalent for each word in a dictionary and substituting it for the original. The real work is to ensure that the intentionality of the translation corresponds to the intentionality of the original phrase.[17]

This ideal is summed up in a highly relevant but unanswerable question: If Jesus could read the Gospels as they are published today, what would he make of them? Just to complicate things a bit further, modern translations generally reflect the Greek originals, but the Greek itself is a report by the evangelists or the Q writer(s) or earlier oral sources of what Jesus said. And since his native language was Aramaic, much of his teaching, especially to the Aramaic-speaking peasants of Galilee, must have been in that language—and the Greek quotations in the Gospel accounts are therefore, like all translations, interpretative renderings. The wide historical range of authors and texts in the rest of the New Testament canon meant that, like the Hebrew scriptures, it had incoherence built into it. Grouping all these texts together and combining them with Jewish writings into a Bible neither overcame their differences nor created an authority that overrides their previous nature. The result has been aptly typified as "concordant discord."[18]

This paradoxical description of the biblical "muck-heap" means that like any garden plot it has to be turned over regularly in order to find and keep what gives nourishment to our lives and imaginations. The labor implicit in a vernacular theology yields fruits unearthed by scholarly investigations into the birth, life, times, environment, deeds, and sayings of Jesus. The results often up-end accepted notions of the imperial nature of God's power as well as religious and secular assumptions about our privileged place in the community of life on Earth. That in turn questions the presumption that the divine order of things authorizes us to live here in ways that take no account of the well-being of other-than-human species.

On the contrary: if Jesus was right, God's concern is focused on those that appear worthless, powerless, and of no account in our eyes. Bruised reeds and smoking flax have no lobbyists working to protect them from economic or ecological hazard. And though science teaches us that the well-being of what we classify as worthless can never be divorced from the good of the whole, Christian dogma has given us a mythic view of Earth as a hierarchical system. According to this organizational chart God rules from the top down: immediately below "Him" stand angels ready to do his bidding, with us below them, and below us all other creatures. At the bottom, furthest from God, is the Earth itself.[19]

To be sure, the angels have pretty much disappeared from this pyramidal imaginary universe, but that has only tended to reinforce the power of those human beings (overwhelmingly male) who can and do claim to exercise power, in God's name, over all the creatures "below" them. This underlying symbolic structure has been built up by and in turn supported the theological muck-heap of traditional Christianity, and with it reinforced the hierarchical structures of Christian churches and governments modeled on and inspired by their imperial foundations.

What holds this conceptual pyramid together is an implied but false relationship between divine and human power that legitimates our dominance over Nature. It also presumes a human independence, based on intelligence or soul, that marks us out and "protects" us from being identified with those "below" us—that is, with Nature. This deep-seated theological understanding of our place in the world has played and continues to play a dominant role in western secular culture where political, economic and dynastic hierarchies mirror this theological structure.

An historical reason for this dominance is religious hierarchies' validation of the exercise of power and consequent violence in the name of God. Public religious ceremonials, such as swearing an oath on the Bible or being crowned in a cathedral, reinforce the (mostly) implicit assumption that the value of a person is in direct relation to a supposed order of nearness to God. Those beings who are deemed most "earthy," that is, most "bodily," occupy the lowest and least valued place in these hierarchies.[20]

Now, however, science is teaching us that in fact it is the other way round. Our existence depends most immediately and definitively on subvisible entities that live at the base of this imagined pyramid. Minute marine algae regulate the formation of clouds that in turn replenish the fresh water supplies on which our daily existence depends. Earthworms ensure the fertility of the soil. Female bodily fertility guarantees the future of all species, including our own. The undeniable facticity of this perspective indicates that the concept of human independence is a political rather than an ecological one.

Neither is independence a viable theological concept. Raking though the hierarchical muck-heap turns up an image of what Paul called "the weakness of God" manifest in the person of Jesus on the cross. This unites him with the "weakness" of human beings in the face of human violence and with our recognized vulnerability to the effects of climate change. An appreciation of this leads to a discussion of how to cultivate peace with unity, for this clearer understanding of our situation calls on us to nurture the intention to live as nonviolently as possible. When done with the whole Earth community in mind, such mindfulness makes an essential contribution to the cultivation of unity. The simple reason is that it orients us toward images of God and responses to God that evoke care for *all things* that have "come to be."

4

SPEAKING THE WORD OF LIFE

> The parable, like other works of art, linguistic and
> visual, can be defined, but only with considerable
> loss. To grasp the parable in its fullness means
> to see what happens when parable occurs, to see
> what happens in the words themselves and to see
> what happens in the horizons circumscribed by
> the parable.
> —Robert W. Funk, *Language, Hermeneutic, and Word of
> God,* p. 126

Parable can take many forms, ranging from a striking or
even shocking story to an image, riddle, or metaphor that
arrests our attention. Whatever form is used it provides us
with an opportunity to arrive at some truth that cannot
be communicated in ordinary prose. Its communicative
power lies in its ability to subvert the expectations of those
attuned to the myth that gives the parable its particular
resonance. In the preceding chapter the book of Jonah
was cited as an example of a parable that challenges not
only the entire prophetic tradition, but the very heart of
the Bible itself: it goes against the Bible *within* the Bible.
Hebrew scholar Herbert Chanan Brichto gives proof of its
subversive character through his commentary and up-to-
date translation of the text:

> The word of YHWH came to Jonah ben-Amittai to this
> effect. "Up! Go to Nineveh—the great city—and pro-
> claim her condemnation. Yes, the indictment against
> them has come up on my docket." Up got Jonah—to

> decamp to Tarsish—in flight from YHWH. He went
> down to Jaffa, found a ship Tarshish-bound. He paid
> the fare and went aboard—with the others Tarshish-
> bound—in flight from YHWH. (Jonah 1:1–3)

One would be hard put to it, says Brichto, to imagine a narrative opening better designed to strike an ancient Israelite audience as discordant, incongruous, perhaps even absurd. A monarch charges his deputy, trusted and long in his service, with a mission that, in the line of his duty, will take him to one end of his lord's far-flung empire. Without a word of demurral, without a suggestion of any motive, the deputy proceeds—ever so casually—to head in the opposite direction. He does not plead unworthiness or superannuation, neither does he beg leave to live out his retirement on his home soil. Instead, he sets out to become an outcast somewhere at the world's end.

As the author intended, Jonah's flight is a *tour de force* of existential absurdity. That is evident in the peremptoriness of the divine command and the prophet's immediate and contrary response. Consider first the threefold repetition of *Tarshish-bound*, and recall that Tarshish, on the westernmost coast of the Mediterranean, represented the far end of the earth, whereas Nineveh lies overland at the eastern boundary of the known world. Note also the repetition of *in flight from YHWH*. Details normally eschewed in terse biblical style—such as finding the right vessel, purchasing a ticket and boarding "with the others" (just another commercial traveler crossing the ocean on the first outward-bound ship)—convey an image of the most obtuse, perplexing and absurd dereliction of duty toward YHWH. Here is a prophet who runs away from God rather than obey his orders! And the crowning, ironic absurdity is that those orders required him to condemn Nineveh for its dereliction of duty to God.[1]

༺༻

Similarly, Jesus' parables do not simply challenge certain aspects of the myth of the kingdom of God. They call upon his hearers to make a judgment about their role in "their lord's far-flung empire" as well as how and by whom they consider it ruled. This means seeing it from the perspective of their own lives and coming to a decision about their activities within it. Like Jonah, they too must decide how to respond to YHWH's commands. And that means opening themselves to new insights about the kind of God who rules this kingdom.

Toward those ends, Jesus used a variety of parables in a variety of ways to shock the imagination of his hearers into a different vision of this kingdom. Among the more noteworthy examples are the Leaven (Matthew 13:33), the Vineyard Workers (Matthew 20:1–15), the Pearl (Matthew 13:45–46), the Mustard Seed (Matthew 13:31b–32), the Buried Treasure (Matthew 13:44), the Dinner Party (Luke 14:16–23//Thomas 64), the Lost Sheep (Matthew 18:12–13), and the Empty Jar (Thomas 97). Set within the context of Jesus' life, these metaphors suggested and still suggest far more than they say. They presented and still present us with visions of the kingdom of God that, through the power of analogical imagination, can change our vision of the contemporary reality of that kingdom. Their revelatory character relies on their being infused, as is the parable of Jonah, with absurdity, realism and relevance. Things that in Jesus' day would have been taken for granted or reckoned of no account—a woman kneading leaven into flour or carrying a jar of meal, a man obeying an order or sowing mustard seed—must instead be carefully assessed and reckoned with.

In parables, as Wilder says, we observe not only human life but nature as well, and thus humanity interacting with nature. The realism of their settings and events portrays a world in which men and women perform customary actions and one thing leads to another. To be sure, the incident may have some seemingly absurd feature: the three measures of meal in which the woman "hides" the leaven is enough to provide bread for some 150 people. Or the parable may focus on some critical life situation, such as the chastisement of the unprofitable servant (Matthew 25:14–30 // Luke 19:12b–27). But they are all true to life— life as lived then and, by analogy, relevant to how we live it now.[2] Buying tickets for a journey may now be done on the Internet, but where and why the buyer intends to travel is still a personal decision. And these choices reflect responses to the forces governing her life, whether economic, familial, or religious.

One of the best known parables is that of the Good Samaritan (Luke 10:30b–35). To understand its relevance it is necessary to know that in Jesus' time the Jewish view of Samaritans would closely resemble our perception of terrorists or insurgents. The shock conveyed to his audience by making such a detestable figure the "hero" of his tale must have been at least as great as that felt by hearers of the story of the disobedient prophet Jonah. Likewise, the image of the "good" Samaritan employs paradox to attack our structure of expectation, but on different grounds. Rather than teaching a lesson about assisting those in distress, which it takes for granted, it demands that we recognize the full and equal humanity of those we have been taught to despise. It thereby challenges us to create a nobler concept of "neighbor."[3]

This involves far more than thinking about the (possible) terrorist next door, though that, too, enters into it. It widens the notion of neighborliness to include not only those near us but those related to us in ways other than mere proximity. Ultimately, it may stretch to (and beyond) all those living in our immediate neighborhood, including its other-than-human inhabitants. This pinpoints what Wilder sees as the combination of "naturalness" or ordinariness in the parables with the deepest mysteries of providence and destiny.

When we hear or read parables today, then, if we grasp them correctly, we, too, are thrown into uncertainty and doubt about their meaning. Or more precisely, we are driven to question why they shock us—or don't. What expectations do we have of ourselves, of our neighbors, of the kingdom of God, and finally, of God? When we reserve our response or, as is more usual, find ourselves incapable of judging what the correct response should be, is it because we no longer know what we should expect of ourselves, of our neighbor, or of God? Parables urge us to pursue such truths as are revealed in them, for these truths are ultimately relevant to our situation here and now.

This follows from the fact that few if any of the recorded parables were originally given applications by Jesus. He may sometimes have called attention to the point of a parable by means of a question or comment, but did not attach allegorical meanings or "morals" to them. Then and now they trigger an internal dialogue that may continue indefinitely; indeed, we may find it impossible to reconcile the contradictory aspects of the parable with any rational sequence of thought or prevailing worldview:

> At its simplest the parable is a metaphor or simile drawn from nature or common life, arresting the hearer by its vividness or strangeness, and leaving the mind in sufficient doubt about its precise application to tease it into active thought.[4]

The myth of the kingdom of God comes alive in parable because the communicative power of the analogy (presenting us simultaneously with the distance of that kingdom from us and its nearness to us) is brought into direct relationship with our present reality. But the difference between that reality and its mythic portrayal as a divine kingdom remains; for we are told that that kingdom is as near and as real as the impure leaven a woman kneads into three measures of meal. At the same time, the presence of the kingdom qualifies and gives another dimension to that reality and to our participatory belonging within it. We see ourselves from a perspective of divine severity and love; but in a way where the deeper dimensions of our character, with its mixture of freedom and helplessness, are married to ordinariness and worldliness.[5]

Dodd points out that our speech is full of "dead" metaphors that have become substitutes for exact thinking. We say that a thought strikes us; that young men sow wild oats, or politicians explore avenues. These tropes are *metaphorically* dead in that they have lost their strangeness and with it the ability to spur us into thought. But this power was and is still alive in Jesus parabolic sayings and stories in that they trigger new ideas by combining images that would not normally be considered together. So they simultaneously astonish and instruct us because surprise plays a decisive role in them. By setting a scene in which an abstract religious concept like kingship or compassion is depicted in secular and concrete but challenging terms, they display the inanimate by means of the animate, making visible the character of possible relationships between us and God.[6]

They also demonstrate that our destiny is at stake in our everyday economic, domestic, and social existence. Parables drawn from nature or common life are told by a lay person, Jesus. They include no sermon, lecture, epic or idealization; no appeal to false mysticism or miracles. The stories work by analogy, compelling us to see things as partly the same and partly different, and on the basis of that difference they lead us to make judgments and come to decisions now. Awareness and conscience are aroused;

we are forced to pay attention, to face things—and urged to change them if need be.

This happens because parables evoke our ordinary daily experience. We can be saved where we are, doing what we do within the sphere of community and family. Within this familiar setting we recognize rich and poor, the honest person and the scoundrel, gaiety and distress, sorrow and thanksgiving. None of this is brought in as scenery nor meant as poetic inspiration. Jesus does not use the details of this world as a springboard but as what they are—our "world."[7] He portrays the Kingdom of God as a set of familiar activities and accepted relationships:

> The kingdom of God is like leaven that a woman took and hid in three measures of meal until the whole was leavened. (Matthew 13:33)

We are presented here with three symbolic images: a woman, some yeast and three measures of flour. There is a single point of comparison, the kingdom of God as leaven. The apparent insignificance of that handful of fungal cells is highlighted by setting it against a vast amount of flour: three measures equals about fifty pounds, or a bushel and a quarter. Some of Jesus' audience might recall that, having offered his three visitors a "morsel" of bread, Abraham ordered Sarah to use "three measures of fine meal" to make cakes for them (Genesis 18:5ff). It was a meal with momentous consequences for both them and their descendants.

The reaction between the yeast and the flour was simply taken for granted in Jesus' day. Today, yeast has been scientifically analyzed and classified as protoctists, nucleated microorganisms that, when brought into contact with plant-derived flour, give rise (literally and figuratively) to new tissues. This process is called *symbiosis,* in which members of different species live in physical contact with each other.[8] Such scientific analyses have revealed some of the mysterious attributes of yeast and of flour that enable them to interact positively and produce what we call bread. Because we can name those attributes and analyze what they do when brought together, they have largely lost their mystery. And with it, we appear to have lost a vital degree of insight into the mystery of the kingdom of God.

But today just as in Jesus' time, the parable insists that the reaction between the leaven and the flour is initiated by and depends on a woman's routine activity: she "conceals," the leaven—that is, she mixes it into the flour. Without human intervention, whether in kitchen, factory, or field, nothing would happen to those ingredients. The power of the yeast, of the kingdom of God itself, is directly linked to what we do. Whether the action takes the form of a daily chore to keep a family alive or as an emergency measure to feed an unexpected guest, the kingdom is made real. Aware of the fundamental role played by bread and hunger in his own life, Jesus anchored the kingdom of God within the domestic setting of an ordinary family kitchen and what happens there.

Our very familiarity with the woman's work gives it its provocative edge. The parable is faithful to things as they are *and*, at the same time, depicts them as greater than or other than they are.[9] In today's more gender sensitive climate, the fact that it is a woman who has the pivotal role may be noted with approval. Not so in the patriarchal culture of Jesus' day. How startling—or indeed shocking—must it have been for him to imply that the advent of the Kingdom of God depends on a female activity?

But the shock goes deeper. The Kingdom actually depends on the leaven: on the hidden power of naturally occurring organisms to combine in certain ways, and through a woman's labor, the products of human toil and life-giving processes in the natural world. And this very basic cultivation of sacred unity happens in order simply to keep the members of her household alive. No Temple, basilica, church, or chapel is required for this activity. The ordinary, the everyday, the natural and familiar features and demands of life are presented as enigmatic disclosures of the Kingdom of God "at home" with us. It exists on earth, and is rooted in the creative powers of soil, plant, and subvisible organism to sustain human life. And it calls upon our ability to work with those powers.

Another religious shock faced members of Jesus' Jewish audience. Leaven was and still is regarded among Jews as a symbol of ritual impurity, of degenerative as well as regenerative power. The original Feast of *Un*leavened Bread marked the beginning of the barley harvest, the first crop to be gathered. For the first seven days of the harvest, only bread made with the new grain was eaten. It was eaten without leaven, that is, without anything from the harvest of the previous year in it. It represented, therefore, a new beginning. The Passover was kept during this same month, at the full moon. Deuteronomy and Josiah's reforms made the Passover a pilgrimage feast, as the feast of the Unleavened bread already was, and the obvious move was to combine the two.

The old rubric about eating unleavened bread at Passover, even though it had nothing to do with the Feast of Unleavened Bread, favored the combination. The text that connects them most closely is Exodus 12, in which the rites for both feasts are incorporated into the Exodus story. Both were celebrated in springtime. For it had been in one springtime long ago that God brought Israel out of Egypt. The feasts of the Passover and of Unleavened Bread commemorate this event.[10]

Contemporary celebrations of Passover weave these two strands of tradition together. The leader points to the *matzah*, or unleavened bread, and asks what it means. A participant replies:

> Of old, *matzah* was meant to recall that the dough pre-
> pared by our people had not time to rise before the final
> act of redemption. "And they baked unleavened cakes
> of the dough since they had been driven out of Egypt
> and could not delay, nor had they prepared provisions
> for themselves." (Exodus 12:39)

> To the driven of the earth we link ourselves today as we
> fulfill the *mitzvah*: "For seven days shall you eat *matzah*,
> that you may remember your departure from Egypt as
> long as you live." (Deuteronomy 16:3)[11]

The sacredness of the *matzah* or unleavened bread is
stressed by an instruction to place three whole pieces in
a special *matzah* cover. They represent the two traditional
loaves set out in the ancient Temple during the festival
day and the extra *matzah* symbolic of Passover. This ritually signifies the mythic sacredness of unleavened bread.
An interesting Christian relic of this custom has been the
use of unleavened bread in the Eucharist, celebrated as the
memorial of Jesus' final Passover.

To say then, as Jesus does, that leaven is a "parable" of
the kingdom of God is to use a familiar but shocking image to portray that kingdom. It speaks of a God identified
not with Exodus and deliverance, or with "high days and
holy days" in the Temple, but with everyday needs and
lives. The kingdom is identified with the mundane, the
earthy and the ordinary. To describe it in these terms is to
do so para-doxically, literally "against teaching," for they
do not allow us to make ordinary sense of what the words
"God" and "leaven" and sacredness' simultaneously hide
and disclose. This "theological muck-heap" or "incarna-
tional linguistic litter" cannot be definitively sorted into its
component parts. Yet taken together, it remains nonsensi-
cal—that is, if it is taken literally.

But its component metaphors of leaven, toil, and
bread do not and are not intended to "make sense" as that

phrase is usually understood. They function by allusion, not analysis; by analogy, not simple similarity. By alluding to one being or entity similar to but belonging within the context of another, they convey information about different dimensions of experience that exceed the terms used. This power of images to disclose truth by allusion resides in poetry, in jokes, in music, in the emotions aroused by beauty in all its visible forms; and in stories that embody ideals like truth-telling, self-sacrifice or love. None of these "add up," yet all of them make our lives not only richer, but possible.

Parables draw us into their world by opening up our world to new meanings. They do so by drawing us into a search for meaning within our lifeworld that discloses new interpretations of it. We may then see their truth more clearly when, as Amos Wilder says, it is set against "the myth of the dispensability of myth, the myth of the denial of myth and the myth of the obsolescence of myth with its stultifying axiom":

> [T]hat genuine truth or insight or wisdom must be limited to that which can be stated in discursive prose, in denotative language stripped as far as possible of all connotative suggestions, in "clear ideas"; in short, in statement or description of a scientific character.[12]

Parable now has to operate against the background of twenty-first century myths of rationalism, positivism, and scientism; of concepts like the social contract, ever-increasing progress, and omni-competent technology. By definition, interpretations and applications of parable were and cannot be fixed and finalized according to any "ism," religious or secular. Yet already in the Synoptic tradition we can see a strong tendency to provide parables with "applications." In the process of handing on the tradition, the horizon of meaning not only tended to become fixed, but to be transmitted along with the parable. In this way the hardening and crystallization of the tradition produced what may be called the loss of interpretative potential. The "openendedness" of the parable that invites the listener to make her own application was and is closed off.[13]

Today, the ways in which we avail ourselves of that openendedness and arrive at more productive interpretations and applications follow the same pattern as in Jesus' time: by being open to and exploring the metaphorical richness of the parable and then relating it to our own situation and audience. Its openendedness remains crucial if we are to see Jesus as the living embodiment of a parabolic encounter between the human and the divine; not the avatar of "either-or," but an ever-present incarnation of "both-and." The role played by metaphor in this encounter is crucial and will be considered in some depth in the following chapter.

5

ENCOUNTERING JESUS

A theory of interpretation which at the outset
runs straight to the moment of decision moves too
fast. It leaps over the moment of meaning, which
is the objective stage. . . . Understanding is not
a "mystical" event, but the result of interpretive
work.
—Paul Ricoeur, *The Conflict of Interpretations*, p. 397

Previous chapters about the relationship between myth
and parable dealt with the pivotal role played by parable
in de-mythologizing the myth to which it is related. It
does this through an internal critique of the literal sense
of myth. The perceived aim of this process is self-understanding leading to a moment of decision. Ricoeur does
not question the aim, but how best to achieve it. It requires
understanding the importance of the metaphoric dimension intrinsic to narrative and ritual forms that include
both myth and parable. Without this framework, parable
would not upset any mythic expectations. For it, too, "calls
up a world"—but one that challenges the world created by
myth.

Understanding a parable's critique of the literal sense of
myth means focusing on their common use of metaphor as
a language form. Mythic and parabolic metaphors connect
us imaginatively to the beginnings of the universe and of
human history. They also connect us to the rhythms of life
and the return of the seasons, to a chain of ancestors, and

to generations of living beings up to and including those of today. Yet for us this metaphoric experience of time past and present is not sequential but simultaneous, not in the past but here and now. Our connections with it occur all at once as we recite or explore the myth or reflect on the parable that challenges it.

This simultaneity offers us a choice as to which of these connections is the focus of our attention. Generally speaking, that choice is made at a subconscious level; and we generally choose those connections that are most familiar to us. The word "familiar" points to the choice most often made: that between and within our own families and cultural traditions.

But within that context, metaphor can also connect us with other times and places by acting as a bridge between what we know and do not know about the world and our place in it. Its power rests on our recognizing, usually subliminally, the difference between our knowledge and our ignorance as well as that between what is true and what is false. At the same time it conveys information to us over and above the terms used. The metaphor "all the world's a stage" assumes an understanding of life in terms of roles, parts, scripts, directors, beginnings, and ends. Simultaneously, the force of the metaphor lies in our knowing that this is not literally true. The world cannot be reduced to a stage for us to strut upon. Therefore, when this (usually) unexpressed acknowledgment of a metaphor's "untruth" is replaced by belief in its *literal* truth, the metaphor is stripped of its "moment of meaning" and loses its power to express our actual experience of the world.

This is especially true of religious metaphors. By saying and singing that "God is our Father" or "God is King" and repeating these formulas over and over in many "sanctified" settings and in many languages, we have bestowed upon these images of God an aura of unquestionable literal truth. As a result, it has become difficult for us to see that *because* such statements are metaphors they disclose the truth that in a literal sense God *is not* our father or a king. Literalism leads us to ignore or be unaware of the "*is not*" pillar holding up the metaphoric bridge of split reference between "father" and "God," between our knowledge of fathers and our ignorance of God.[1] This would effectively amount, as Ricoeur says, to "leaping over the moment of meaning" that occurs when we take on the interpretive work and intentional analysis of a narrative text.

That work and analysis is now metaphorically described as "de-construction," the process of breaking down a mythic or parabolic passage into its constituent elements of assertion and denial and examining them in order to understand and decide what to do with what they disclose. It is that moment of disclosure that connects us metaphorically to the world-of-the-text and through this connection evokes existential decision. This process of de-mythologizing (as in de-literalizing the metaphor "God is our Father") requires both understanding and acknowledging the fact that myth relates us symbolically to a larger referential framework—one to which we may or may not be able to relate our own experience. If, for instance, we cannot agree with the positive aspects of the metaphor, we may feel the parabolic shock of the *is not* factor that is the "moment of meaning."

Poets are experts at delivering this shock:

"The child is father to the man"
How can he be? The words are wild.
Suck any sense from that who can
(G.M. Hopkins, "The Child is Father to the Man")

Spring is like a perhaps hand
(which comes carefully
out of Nowhere)
(e.e. cummings, "Spring is like a perhaps hand")

> Jesus says: If two make peace with one another in one and the same house, (then) they will say to the mountain: "Move away," and it will move away. (Thomas 48)

Reading these as metaphors, we begin to perceive the difference between the logical effects of myth and of parable. According to Funk myth's logic—that is, its use of language—presupposes that the meaning of words such as "child," "father," "Spring," or "mountain" is constant. Myth directs attention one way and not another, reinforcing a particular meaning through ritual enactment and consequently narrowing and restricting the totality of references available. In direct contrast, parabolic use of metaphor, as in the parable of Jonah or of the leaven, opens up potential for new meaning *within the mythic context* by means of imaginative shock. Its impact encompasses not just this or that attribute or interpretation, but the surrounding whole. It presents itself differently if focalized in this or that other thing or event.[2]

Jesus' perception and preaching of the kingdom of God was expressed at a time when his lifeworld was dominated by the mythic imperial power of Caesar's surrogate, Herod Antipas. Within that *koinon*, dominant images of the fatherhood of God and of the kingdom of God were encapsulated in a coinage issued by Caesar bearing his likeness and the legend DIVI F that identified him as DIVI FILIUS, the SON OF GOD. Inasmuch as this image of God was the one imposed and generally accepted in Jesus' lifetime, how could it not affect his and his audience's perceptions of God, as Father or King? In fact, many were scandalized by what he himself said and did (Matthew 11:25). To say: Blessed are you poor: God's kingdom is yours! (Q/Luke 6:20–21; Matthew 5:1–4, 6), contradicts the common mythic or accepted expectations of that kingdom. Its inversion of all normal images of kingship, whether human or divine, delivers an imaginative shock that opens up the mind to new horizons of meaning and possibilities for decisive acting.

Walter Brueggemann discerns this shock and its effects in the Jewish prophetic critique of accepted notions of kingship and kingdom. He notes its contemporary resonance in civil rights movements within African American churches and in liberation resistance groups in Latin America. By ridiculing the prevailing culture in their cultic events, they turn both history and its meaning upside down. Funeral becomes festival, grief becomes doxology, and despair turns to amazement. Perhaps the rite is no more than a cultic event, but it may also be the symbolic dramatization of an inversion of power that "kings" and "the grim royal middle class" do not believe possible. And it is the inversion that surprises people who are powerless.

> Inversions are not easy, not without cost, and never neat and clear. But we ought not underestimate the power of the poet. Inversions may begin in a change of language, a redefined perceptual field or altered consciousness. So his poetry speaks about the inversion even in exile and the images tumble out.[3]

When the new king rules, says Brueggemann, it is "new song time" (Isaiah 42:10). The old songs had to be sung in the presence of mockers (Psalm 137:3), but new song time is a way to sing a new social reality; and freedom songs have stood behind every freedom act. New song time is when a new covenant inaugurates this new mode of reality.[4] In singing *"We shall overcome"* and *"We shall all be free,"* we resonate with the spirit of such inaugurations.

As Funk notes, Wilder is on the mark when he says that Jesus, without explicitly saying so, *shows* that for him human destiny is at stake in all aspects of our ordinary creaturely existence: ecological, domestic, economic and social. When Jesus speaks of a lost sheep, a mustard seed, a banquet, or "some other commonplace," the hearer senses

without prompting that more is intended than a pleasant
or amusing anecdote:

> The parabolic imagery lays bare the structure of hu-
> man existence that is marked by convention, custom,
> consensus. It exposes the "world" in which man is
> enmeshed and to which and for which he must give ac-
> count. It is this element of ultimate seriousness that is
> implicit in the patent everydayness of the parable. The
> "field" that the parable conjures up is not merely this or
> that isolated piece of earthiness, but the very tissue of
> reality, the nexus of relations that constitutes the arena
> of human existence where life is won or lost.[5]

௸

Can one then see Jesus himself as a parable? Amos Wilder
claims that parables are the counterpart of Jesus' own person and presence among us: not as a philosopher, priest, or
scribe but as an artisan; not in the desert or in the temple
but in the marketplace. To know who Jesus was, he says,
it is not enough to ask what he said, or he is reported to
have said, about himself or his mission. In his modes of
speech we may recognize yet another clue to the mystery
of his being. It is as though many ancient tributaries of
speech and style merged in him. We find the parable of
the wisdom tradition at home in his speech as well as the
prophetic oracle.[6]

His parables then become an expression of the mystery
he embodies, a mystery that is "nothing but the hidden
dawn of the kingdom of God itself amidst a world that to
human eyes gives no sign of it."[7] In John's Gospel such a
meeting between this world and the kingdom of God embodied in Jesus occurs when a Samaritan woman comes to
draw water at a well. Surprised to find Jesus sitting there,
she is even more surprised when he, a Jew, asks her to give
him some water to drink (John 4:3–8). The naturalness of

his need for a drink provokes the shock of a Jewish man asking a despised Samaritan for one. John's account continues with a progressively more shocking series of actions and dialogues. They present us with a Jesus who not only flouts the normal traditions and codes of conduct of his own people, but at the same time knowingly flouts hers. She asks: "How is it that you, a Jew, ask a drink of me, a woman of Samaria?" Jews, the narrator explains, have no dealings with Samaritans. A Samaritan woman did not expect a Jew to ask her for help, just as nobody in Jesus' Jewish audience who heard the parable of the Samaritan expected that "one of those people" would aid the presumably Jewish victim of a robbery.

The basis for discrimination was reinforced by the fact that Samaritan women were considered by Jews as doubly unclean—indeed the very embodiment of uncleanness. They were seen as "menstruants from the cradle," that is, always; and their husbands were perpetually unclean for the same reason. Any place where a Samaritan lay down was levitically unclean, and a traveler through Samaritan territory who accepted food or drink from them could never know if it was clean or not. By the same rule, the spittle of a Samaritan woman was unclean—as would be her drinking vessel also.[8]

Jesus responds by saying that if she knew who was talking to her, she would ask him for living water and he would give it to her. She misunderstands him: the well is deep, he has no jar; how would he get the water? Is he greater than Jacob who gave the well to the Samaritans? Jesus replies that whoever drinks from the well will become thirsty again, but whoever drinks the water that he will give will never thirst. The woman then asks him for this water in order "that I may not thirst, nor come here to draw."

The geography of the story places the well at about a mile from the nearest city, and their encounter takes place at the sixth hour—noon—in the heat of the day. Jesus' thirst unites him with despised classes, women and Samaritans, who have to come to the well during such un- social hours to keep thirst at bay.

He tells her to call her husband and she replies that she has none. Jesus agrees: he informs her that she has had five and the man she is presently living with is not her husband. She realizes that he knows things about her even though they had never met before and responds to his un- canny knowledge by acknowledging him as a prophet. The ensuing conversation between them contains some of the most profound statements recorded in the Gospels. Jesus states that the Father is to be worshipped in spirit and in truth, and that God is spirit; she confesses Jesus to be the Messiah, and he receives and endorses her confession.

When the disciples return they are astonished to find him talking to a woman. In fact, they are struck dumb, for to engage in conversation with a female stranger, and a Samaritan to boot, was grossly improper. This is not how they expect Jesus to behave! Nonetheless, the evangelist says, they refrained from asking him such embarrassing questions as "What do you want?" or "Why are you talking with *her*?" She, on the contrary, is stirred into action; she proclaims Jesus to be the Christ. She leaves her water jar, goes to the city and says to those she encounters, "Come, see a man who told me all I ever did. Can this be the Messiah?" (John 4:1–29).

The evangelist tells us that the encounter with Jesus forces her, and subsequently her fellow Samaritans, to re- assess their beliefs and codes of conduct; in fact he claims that "many Samaritans believed in him because of the woman's witness" (John 4:39). The Greek word here trans- lated "witness" had already been used of John the Baptist (John 1:7). C. K. Barrett comments that to bear witness is the task of a disciple. By the time John's Gospel was written, then, the Samaritan woman had been ranked with John the Baptist as witness and disciple, and as such took precedence over the apostles. This encounter may then also be read as an account of the foundation of the flourishing Samaritan church recorded in Acts 8.[9]

> Now when the apostles at Jerusalem learned that Samaria had accepted God's message, they sent Peter and John to visit them. After the two had arrived, they prayed that the converts might receive the Holy Spirit, for the Spirit had not yet fallen upon any of them. They had merely been baptized in the name of the Lord Jesus. (Acts 8:14)

The preceding verses (Acts 8:5–8) give an account of Philip's mission in Samaria in which he told the Samaritans about the Messiah and about God's reign. This had led to their being baptized. The narrative, says Pervo, had given no hint that that baptism was defective and needed to be supplemented by apostolic prayer. Readers are also free to infer that the defining gift of the Spirit required the imposition of apostolic hands. Yet the initial gift of the Spirit had come without reference to baptism, as in Jerusalem (Acts 2:1–4); or prior to Cornelius's baptism (Acts 10:44–46).

> The patent fact is that the Spirit comes at the opportune moment. Behind this literary device is a theological conviction: the wind blows where it wills. No institution or person can manipulate the Spirit of God, a point doubly made in this passage.[10]

This is the Spirit of *koinonia*, already manifest in Jesus' encounter with a Samaritan woman: "The time is coming, and *now is*, when true worshippers worship the Father in spirit and in truth" (John 4:23). Jesus proclaimed this after she had reminded him that "Jews have no dealings with Samaritans," and after he had affirmed her belief that "salvation is from the Jews." (John 4:22). Similarly, in his encounter with Cornelius, Peter repeats the *koinon* against

Jews consorting, eating, or drinking with Samaritans or gentiles (Acts 10:28). In both cases, the Spirit of *koinonia* recognizes man-made religious, social and political boundaries—only to abolish them.

ॐ

While providing a clear and startling example of the discipleship of both sexes established by Jesus, his parabolic encounter with the Samaritan woman also records the imaginative shock that opened the disciples' minds to the Spirit of *koinonia* manifest in his actions—and led to Peter's eventual conversion to it. Taken in conjunction with Matthew 25:34–46, this encounter is a profound challenge to those who see themselves as entitled by birth, gender, or ecclesiastical office to identify with Jesus and to tell others what it means to be identified as his disciple.

For later generations of Christians the normative mode of encounter with Jesus is through the written word, and follows from the kind of interpretive work that leads to what Ricoeur calls "the moment of decision." A pivotal moment in this development occurred in Europe when, due to a proliferation of translations into vernacular languages, "the Bible burst on the sixteenth century with the force of a revelation." We are so used to having shelfloads of Bibles in every known language that it is hard for us to imagine a time when "the Word of God was experienced as a hurricane turning the world upside down" and Scripture could be read and seen to have immediate and urgent implications for everything from the most intimate of personal concerns to the entire ordering of society.[11]

The impact of individual access to Scripture on orthodox interpretations was varied, and typically depended on whether its message was being embraced by individuals and groups or by governments that adapted it to promote their nationalist or state-building agenda. There is a precedent for this response in the insistence in Jerusalem that the Samaritans who had received the Word of God must be baptized in the Spirit through the laying on of apostolic hands (Acts 8:14–18). It is noteworthy that Simon the magician, already established in Samaria, tried to access this exercise of spiritual power by offering to buy it from the apostles. Transactions of this kind were later named and condemned as "simony."

So the Catholic Church responded with considerable suspicion to the advent of individual access to Scripture. And even Protestant groups soon began to feel threatened by such exegetical freedom.

> Equally critical was the relationship between Scripture and Church, or rather Churches. The latter sought to ensure, although with varying degrees of success, that Scripture was read through the lenses of their approved theologians, preachers and teachers; their catechisms, liturgies, councils and creedal confessions . . . What one party saw as the Scriptural renewal of the Church and its sacraments was viewed by others as its ruin.[12]

By the year 1500, however, the Bible was no longer a mere tool in the hands of institutions like Church or State. A new actor had swept onto the stage: the printing press. For Luther, it was "the latest and greatest gift of God," and by the time of his death in 1546 some 100,000 copies of his German translation of the New Testament had poured out from Wittenberg alone. Such access to biblical texts constituted a radical empowerment of ordinary people, giving them the means and authority to ask awkward and probing questions. Jesus' interrogation by the Samaritan woman was replicated in the privacy of people's homes, in taverns, and in formally staged civic disputes. The Catholic Cochlaeus complained that the New Testament was so commonly available "that even tailors and cobblers, even women and other simple folk [sic] who had only learnt to read a little German" were reading it with great enthusiasm while others "carried it around pressed to their bosom, and learnt it by heart."[13]

The prejudices of the apostles resurface in such statements, but with an added factor: what sixteenth-century lay people now could read in—or read into—biblical texts, might and often did conflict with what they heard during public worship. Sermons were often interrupted. Angry French and Scottish women were known to hurl their stools at preachers when provoked. Moreover, when the Bible was championed as the supreme authority for faith and life, this not only made the reform of the Church inevitable, but potentially threatened every custom and institution in secular society. Family life, gender norms, and Church-State relations all had to be revisited. Scriptural blueprints loomed large in the popular as well as the scholarly imagination.

This impacted on the *koinon* in its secular as well as its ecclesiastical form. Jesus' encounter with the Samaritan woman and its influence on the Church in Samaria shines through in Matheson's account of a young Bavarian mother, Argula von Grumbach. For her, Scripture was a source of light and joy, sweeping her on from one text to the next. The biblical preaching that she heard and the pamphlets from Wittenberg she devoured spurred her into a disciplined study of Scripture that revolutionized her life:

> The wall of separation between private and public collapsed. "Dr Martin" had opened up for her with his translation of Scripture a quite new understanding of God, Church and Society. As "a mere woman" she proceeded to launch a frontal attack on the Old Church, starting with the prestigious theology faculty in Ingolstadt. She launched a swingeing critique of Bavaria's legal, educational and patronage systems and questioned both the traditional understanding of

women and the mores of her own class, the nobility. What gave her a voice was the printing press. What made her audience sit up and take notice was her mastery of Scripture.[14]

Matheson describes this as the "subversive and programmatic impact of Scripture." Since von Grumbach, such personal voyages of discovery and self-discovery have flowed from a disciplined study of the recorded conversations between Jesus and others. Its challenges to the *koinon* have revealed the paradoxical God of *koinonia* present and acting in Jesus and disclosed in his parables. This is what I take Eberhard Jüngel to mean when he integrates the person with the parable by saying that the parable "collects" Jesus, his relationship to God, his eschatology, his ethic, *and* the hearer into a language event that is the kingdom of God.[15]

But I would make an important qualification to this: Jesus is *a* parable of God, not *the* parable. To make that absolutist claim would be to limit God's ability to reveal Godself at all times, in manifest ways, and in parables in every language, culture and place throughout Earth's history. Other religions and peoples have also used myth and parable to speak of and to their deities. This truth must be acknowledged, for, as Gerhard Ebeling remarks, if the language of faith is to be in harmony with Jesus, then it must have an unreserved obligation to tell the truth; it must give unlimited scope for the truth.[16] That includes the truth that people of other religions, or those with none, also have the capacity to experience and disclose the truth in their beliefs.

Having said that, it is Jesus who for me embodies the iconic aspect of metaphor, showing us transcendent divinity through a socially insignificant human personality: that of a Galilean Jewish peasant.[17] The embodying of God in a weary, unclean, thirsty, and compassionate human being is a scandal to religious conservatives, an offense to rational thinkers, and a reversal of our expectations as to who embodies and wields divine power.

As an "active metaphor for God" Jesus was and remains a scandal to those who look for a mythic image of divine power. Before his crucifixion, it is his shocking, parabolic presence and actions that arrest our attention and retain the power to tease us into further thought. They show us that human destiny is at stake in our ordinary creaturely existence and activities—earthy, biodiverse, political and religious.

The link, the human earthly continuity between Jesus and the Christ, rests on two important levels of understanding implicit in seeing him as a parable of God. First, the mythic understanding of "God in heaven" cannot be divorced from Jesus' earthly identity. But that identity cannot be detached from his human ancestry. Second, his human identity cannot be detached from a Jewish mythic understanding of the Messiah (the Christ). The continuity of both inheritances is integral to the paradoxical claim that the human being called Jesus *is* the Messiah or the Christ.

But his *non-identity* with this mythic figure, attested by those who shared these inheritances, is summed up in their poignant remark: "We had hoped that he was the one to liberate Israel" (Luke 24:21). Plainly, to them he was *not* that one. This literal identity *was not* held to by the majority of Jews and others—neither soon after his death nor up to the present day. Nevertheless, like Ricoeur, a deeply Christian thinker, we may and indeed must insist on the continuity and identity of the earthly Jesus and the Christ. Ricoeur directs attention to a place and time after Jesus' death when his earthly identity as a preacher not only developed into preaching about him but about the identity between him and the Messiah. Ricoeur traces this development through to the Pauline proclamation or *kerygma*, which stands as a definitive moment in *identifying* the Jesus of the Gospels with the Messiah (Christ) of the Jewish Scriptures.

> For I delivered to you as of first importance what I also received, that Christ died for our sins in accordance with the scriptures, that he was buried, that he was raised on the third day in accordance with the scriptures and that he appeared to Cephas, then to the twelve. Then he appeared to more than five hundred brethren at one time, most of whom are still alive, though some have fallen asleep. Last of all, as to one untimely born, he appeared also to me. (1 Corinthians 15:3–8)

This proclamation of Jesus as the Christ has, however, been preached as if Jesus *lost* his human identity with us when he was raised as the Christ. This is what I deduce from Ricoeur's insistence that if that proclamation does not include Jesus' earthly *past* in Christ's *present*, then it runs the risk of interpreting the latter in the sense of a Hellenistic myth. This happens if and when Jesus is understood *only* "according to the scriptures" and in terms of transfer from the old to the new. Then he becomes "the exegesis and exegete of Scripture."[18]

It is also true, of course, that being human is the only reality we can speak about with any certainty or authority. We exist within the complex unity of relationships, both human and other-than-human, that constitute our existence and identity. As did Jesus. If we forget that, then his distance from today's scientific and historical culture appears as an original distance, a difference in origins from us.[19] Then cultivating unity with him and within the whole of our everyday creaturely existence is not possible. But if we remember that we share our earth identity and ancestry with him, then, as we shall see in the next chapter, unity with him calls for more than a rejection of the *koinon* of violent imperialism. It calls for an active cultivation of peace.

6

EARTH IDENTITY

A community's ways of identifying the
individual, then, meet more or less successfully
the individual's ways of identifying himself
with others.
—E. H. Erikson, *Identity,* p. 160

While an historical distance of about two thousand years separates Jesus from ourselves, it is not a static space, but one filled with centuries of human cultural achievements, geographical discovery, space exploration and scientific breakthroughs. All these have enlarged and deepened our understanding of what it means to be human. When we say that Jesus is human we usually mean that he is the same sort of creature as we are, that he is "one of us." Therefore, much of what we have discovered about our own identity during those two thousand years applies equally to his. Like ours, his rests on the sameness (*idem*) of being (*ens*) that we share as members of the human species. No matter how far back in human history an individual lived, we take for granted that an essential and existential form of identity connects us and that person. This is as true of the person of Jesus twenty centuries ago as it is for those alive with us today.

More usually, however, we identify ourselves by stressing our distinctness from others rather than our sameness with them: we focus on *who* we are as distinct from *what* we are. This affirms our selfhood as an individual.[1] In western industrialized societies this sense of isolated individuality

87

has been cultivated to such an extent that we find it difficult not only to identify with members of our own species outside our family or nation, but also to remember that our species is but one among, and not separate from, all others that make up the community of life on earth.

A major reason for this memory loss can be traced historically to the continuing rise in European thought of individualism: a self-perspective definitively proposed by Thomas Hobbes as that of a "war of all against all." Human beings, he said, are naturally pure, relentless egoists who can be brought to live in harmony only by fear of the threatening power of government. And they are required to obey it only insofar as it protects their lives. The more awkward side of this tacit social contract is that if it is to work, each individual citizen must be considered as wholly separate, as a unity devoted to its own interests and safety. Any outside obligation, any possible social claim—and thus all morality—is valid only insofar as it serves that ruling purpose.[2] Current "Tea Party" rhetoric in America shows that this type of individualism is alive and well today.

Environmental, religious, and educational factors have reinforced this isolationist self-understanding, both personally and as a species. Material and technological progress over the past two centuries has industrialized and urbanized societies worldwide, isolating large numbers of their human populations from immediate contact with other species. Within those societies, religious teachings have reinforced the presupposition that each and every member of the human species, by virtue of species membership alone, has a special ontological status relative to other living beings or animals.[3] Linked to this, we have learned to see human intelligence not as organically linked to the material world, but as something separate, higher, and extraneous—a quality belonging to an alien spiritual tribe called on to depersonalize, exploit, and colonize the natural world.[4]

As a result of these cultural trends, we routinely identify ourselves as unique individuals within a unique species, and this self-appraisal has real consequences for ourselves and for the community of life as a whole. Cultivating a sense of our unity with it, within it, and beyond it with other species has become increasingly difficult even as we accumulate scientific evidence for this unity of being. Science has definitively shown that all forms of life on earth today, including ours, had a common beginning in one type of cell that arose in the oceans perhaps as long ago as 3.8 billion years. That is the moment *when all things began* for those living today and from which we can trace our common ancestry with all living species.[5]

It is also the baseline for the *koinonia* of our existence, for our mutual sharing of and participating with all other earthly beings in using and contributing to Earth's common resources. This understanding of our unity with them has in a very real sense been cultivated by digging into fossil records and using sophisticated technologies to explore the physical and genetic lineage of as many as possible of our ancestors, and thereby finding links between human and pre-human life. We are slowly learning how to cultivate further insights into those findings and to base moral imperatives on them; in effect, we are beginning to unify our understanding of *what* we are with *who* we are today. For this emerging and counter-cultural view of ourselves as a species has many implications for our self-understanding and conduct. It affects the manner of our relationships within what we have belatedly begun to recognize as the "common-unity" of life on earth. Increasing recognition of this interconnectedness is now reinforced by imaginative, multi-media reconstructions of our evolutionary inheritance. An example is David Attenborough's television programme *First Life* (BBC 2010).

In line with this, the religious concept of *koinonia,* as in Peter's vision, must expand to carry the dual sense of what is common to us as individuals within our species and what we hold in common as an earth community. This double aspect of individual gifts and shared goods allows us to use the word *koinonia* personally and collectively. Personally, we share individually the same type of earthly existence as all other human beings. And as a species we share with all others the resources that sustain this existence. Personally, we are vulnerable to those "warlike" human characteristics in other individuals invoked by Hobbes. Collectively, we share the vulnerability of all earthly species to the effects of our actions and theirs. These range from the implied threat of nuclear annihilation to the gradual erosion of Earth's resources through the escalating consumerism of an increasing human population. Added to this are the global effects of human-induced climate change.

Sad to say, these effects to a large extent characterize the present impact of our species on the whole community of life on Earth. They also broadly define the tasks implicit in cultivating unity, since in common with all other species we depend on the same earthly resource base. All contribute to it and expect to be able take from it what they need to maintain their lives. So our primary concern is for members of our own species who, for a variety of reasons, are unable to satisfy their needs. The theological metaphor commonly used for sharing with them is *koinonia* understood as a visible gift response, sometimes to a direct request and other times to an unspoken but perceived need. So Jesus said to the Samaritan woman, "Give me a drink" (John 4:7). And Paul writes of going to Jerusalem "with aid among the saints, for Macedonia and Achaia have made *koinonian* (gifts) for the poor there" (Romans 15:26).

But in fact, given what has been said about our shared resource base, we all live in *koinonia* by participating in and contributing to the common goods that are Earth's gifts and sharing them with others.[6] Basic gifts to us include such "natural goods and services" as pollination, medicines, fertile soils, clean air, and water. Together they sustain our familial, economic, political, and religious institutions. As gifts from and within the whole Earth community they exist above and beneath, within and beyond human social and national borders as well as those of the Internet's virtual communities. From this perspective, the term *koinonia* is evolving culturally to mean that we live by participating in, cultivating, appreciating, and caring for the gifts of the whole community of life. Furthermore, it implies that meeting the needs of future communities depends on present cultivation of our common resource base. *Koinonia* no longer simply describes what we share with Jesus and with that first community of his followers in Jerusalem. Its meaning has expanded to encompass our table fellowship with their ancestors and ours; with all those species that formed and sustained the environments in which their lives flourished or flagged as do ours; and with the cultivation and conservation of future resources for those individuals and species yet to come into being.

This understanding is a benchmark in our scientific and cultural awareness of the network of causality that connects us with our past, with our environments, and with the future wellbeing of all creatures. The essentially reciprocal nature of all these relationships has become ever clearer and is now taken for granted as an overarching principle in the routine understanding and use of such terms as symbiosis, biodiversity, organism, ecology, climate, and environment. The catch-all phrase *conditions of existence* is now understood to extend beyond personal access to food, air, warmth, and water to include all those variations in weather covered by the term *climate* and our contributions to it. Some of those, such as carbon dioxide emissions, remain as invisible to the naked eye as they were in the time of Jesus. But our modern technologies can quantify them, pinpoint their origins, and monitor their effects around the globe.

This has led to our reluctant acceptance that, as a species, our choice of lifestyles no longer affects one particular place, social group, or resource base alone. Nevertheless, as Ramon Panikkar points out, the presuppositions about lifestyle or development among those that contribute to or measure their impact remain largely unchanged or unchallenged:

> It is usually left out of consideration in statistical studies on poverty and "underdevelopment" that the "developed" model cannot serve as one on a world scale. If the whole world had the same number of automobiles per capita or consumed the same quantity of paper or electricity as the developed countries, life on the planet would be ecologically unviable beyond the twenty-first century, speaking very optimistically. The average citizen of a developed country consumes fifty times as much energy as one in a moderately developed country. The arithmetic is easy: earth does not offer all this.[7]

Fifteen years after Panikkar succinctly expressed this truth, we in developed countries find it just as difficult, indeed almost impossible to accept or adjust to the "arithmetic" of our lifestyles. We struggle to overcome a deeply entrenched and culturally endorsed individualism that not only ignores or actively rejects current scientific research on this topic, but also resists a slowly growing body of ecological assessments based on it. The inescapable sum exacted from the resources of the whole Earth community by our lifestyles represents both our ineluctable connection to that community and our harmful impact on it.

This in turn reveals the unpalatable fact that the Gaian evolution that preceded our emergence as a species and maintains our existence can and presumably will carry on without us. That reinforces an earlier lesson from cosmology implicit in the work of Copernicus and Galileo and immediately rejected because it revealed a similarly unpalatable truth: that just as Earth is not at the centre of the universe, neither are we. Nor, most importantly, is any particular group of us.

Our true place in the universe was established by Darwin, who identified us as just one among the countless forms of life that have evolved and are still evolving on this planet—and as far as we know, on it alone. While he saw "grandeur" in this view of life, most of his contemporaries saw it as robbing us of any grandeur. In particular, it robbed us of our religious grandeur. No longer might we assume that our species had been specially created by God to rule all others. Nor could non-believers assume our right to do so on the grounds of our superior intelligence, our lethal use of force, or our advanced technologies.[8]

A further deepening of this perspective that sees us as having no important differences from other living beings (and so further reversing our sense of human privilege) has come from the discovery of "deep time:" time in the biologically and geologically distant past. This refers to and explores continuous interactions between living organisms and their environments that have evolved over billions of years. It shows us that the ability of any terrestrial organism—including ourselves—to emerge, increase, and spread geographically is limited by and dependent on environmental factors, particularly the availability of natural resources and energy capacity.[9]

Within that understanding of our origins, of the "original" gift of life and what sustains it, is an ever-increasing understanding of what it means to be human. In other

words, that we can properly place and read human history—and Jesus' history—only within the global context of
Earth's history, a continuum that began nearly 13.7 billion
years ago when the Universe literally began creating itself.
It formed strings of galaxies, in one of which, the Milky
Way, gravity drew together clouds of interstellar dust and
gases, and gave birth to the Sun. Then, a little over 9 billion
years later, some 4.5 billion years ago, it fused debris cir-
cling that nascent Sun into our Earth, a planet spun from
dust and rock whose life was nourished and continues to
be nourished by the Sun's warmth:

> All sides bask in its blessings, but none bake excessively:
> we are not toasted to a turn. Likewise the distance of the
> Earth from the Sun is finely adjusted—not so close that
> we are burned, nor yet so far that the rays from the Sun
> would be too dim to allow the chemical reactions upon
> which life depends.[10]

Our position on Earth is finely calibrated with Earth's
position in regard to the Sun. This energy source has been
called "the common root" of all life, for it initiated the evolutionary processes that continue to occur within whole
ecosystems and include our relationships with other organisms and with each other. These scientific revelations make
it theoretically and physically impossible for us to claim
pole position in the evolution of life or to be an exception
to evolutionary rules. Accepting the implications of this
truth and acting accordingly is what I call ecological hu-
mility. It means accepting the fact that we cannot exempt
ourselves from participation in the mutuality and vulnerability of gift exchange, nor from the power of death and
change—though we may act as though we can.

☙

These conditions characterized Jesus' life also. They both
made it possible and identifiably human—that is, depen-

dent on others with whom he shared the "natural goods and services" of the planet. He also inherited and shared in communal cultural and religious myths. As an individual he participated in a community of life without which he could not have existed, and like all within it he was subject to the power of death and change. This narrative account of his birth, life and death is not couched in biblical language but informed by contemporary western culture; not recited in cathedrals but informed by lessons learnt in universities, schools, and laboratories; not required reading in theological research departments but fundamental to contemporary understanding of all those who have lived before us as well as of those alive now.

The most important historical statements about Jesus' identity are those made by Pilate presenting him to the crowd as "a man" (*idou ho anthropos!*) and his later identification as "the Son of God" (*ton huiou tou theou*) by the Christian bishops at Nicaea in June of 325 CE, summoned there from every part of the Empire by Constantine,

> [to] consolidate the Church, which represented in his eyes the spiritual aspect of his empire, on the basis of the widest possible measure of doctrinal unity.[11]

Pilate's statement signals imperial power over life and death; the *koinon* of war and conquest, of victory and defeat that identifies self and other, enemy and friend, rebellion and order—and is played out by colonizer and colonized alike. It also marks the moment when the *koinonia* founded on Jesus' vision of God was confronted with but not overcome by imperial power.

Nicaea signals the moment when that *koinonia* was made subject to the imperial *koinon* of doctrinal unity. Within that framework the bishops identified Jesus as

> one Lord Jesus Christ, the Son of God, begotten from the Father, only-begotten, that is, from the substance of the Father, God from God, light from light, true God

from true God, begotten not made, of one substance
with the Father through Whom *all things came into being*; things in heaven and things on earth (my italics).[12]

Nicaea was significant in the "unearthly" language
used to describe Jesus, his ancestry and his relationship
with God. It also signaled a radical transformation in our
perception of the Spirit manifest in his life. That perception deteriorated from a *koinonia* based on his cultivation
of peace through nonviolent relationships with others
toward a *koinon* based on the imperial power of militarism
and characterized by the violence of war and continuous
conflict. Failure to be baptized meant disenfranchisement
and virtual outlawry. Citizenship and being a Christian
were now synonymous.[13]

This shift from peace to war has meant a shift in identity for Christians: new definitions of enemy and friend;
of who defends and who attacks; of who deserves compassion and who should gain victory. The "good" are located
"high" in the social order, whereas the bad belong to the
bottom. This world view has become deeply ingrained in
western civilization.[14]

All of which was foreshadowed, indeed was boasted of
by Eusebius in his account of the imperial banquet held to
celebrate the conclusion of the Nicene Council:

Detachments of the body guard and troops surrounded
the entrance of the palace with drawn swords, and
through the midst of them the men of God (the bishops) proceeded without fear into the innermost of the
Imperial apartments, in which some were the emperor's
companions at table while others reclined on couches
arranged on either side. One might have thought that
a picture of Christ's kingdom was thus shadowed forth.

Dominic Crossan, radically opposed to this image of the
kingdom proclaimed by Jesus, asks who other than an imperialist Christian could have thought that this was a pic-

ture of the messianic banquet foreshadowed in Jesus' table fellowship with the poor, with women, with the outcast and the sinner?[15]

From Nicaea onwards the imposition of doctrinal unity, if necessary by drawn swords, became the *koinon* of Christianity. Cultivating it and/or destroying it through force forms a more or less continuous sequence in church history, notably from the break between the Eastern and Western Churches through to the Crusades and on to the civil wars that raged in Europe from the fifteenth century onwards. From then on doctrinal struggles also configure European colonization of the Americas. Theologically and symbolically, this strand of violence can be traced through an iconography of salvation that centers on representing Jesus as a militant and victorious savior figure.[16]

Wherever it occurs, this recourse to violence reflects an imperial *koinon* imposed "from above" in the name of a divine ruler (Caesar) or of a *Divi Filius* (Son of God). By contrast, the *koinonia* that characterized Jesus' relationships came "from below" and was cultivated in the name of the God who created "all things good," and who cares for them "without discrimination." Where Caesar was mediator or model, he acted as either supreme warlord or peacemaker in order to *make* Jews and Galatians *one* in himself. In the messianic *koinonia*, unity in the name of the God of Jesus *created* a civic and religious space where, mindful of his command to love our enemies, Jesus the Jew could ask a Samaritan woman for a drink, and a colonized Jew, Peter, could offer peace to the colonizer Cornelius—and have it gratefully accepted:

> Such a universalism "from below" was incompatible with the principles of imperial universalism "from above." It announced a new relationship between self and other based on universal solidarity rather than on competition and warfare. It did not simply abrogate

imperial religion. It abrogated the logic of battle as the foundation of world order.[17]

If only! Even as I quote Brigitte Kahl, I am struck by the irony of her words. Hobbes' theory of individualism was, as he saw it, a rational response to an ongoing series of civil wars that were nominally wars of religion between Christians. He couldn't stand seeing people deceived by pious nonsense into fighting battles that didn't concern them and ending up dead. He wanted what he saw as a state of continual war by all (individuals) against all (individuals) loaded in favor of the individual. Therefore he proposed a civil contract between government and individuals for the protection of their own lives—and only for that. But for that to work, each individual citizen had to be considered as wholly separate. Any outside obligation, whether to God or other people, would weaken the self-preservative motive upon which the contract depends.[18]

Today we live with and either implicitly or explicitly endorse this variation on the imperial *koinon*. It is the type of religious "unity" Kahl talks about when she says that it turns self against other in "endless spirals of violence, competition and oppression."[19] For the most part, being Christian has become a powerful and loaded distinction between *who* we are (religiously) as individuals and *what* we are as a species. This latter, our earth identity, has been ignored to such a degree that endless spirals of violence, competition, and oppression associated with war have produced effects *on* Earth that remain largely ignored. If these effects *are* assessed, it is in terms of economic advantage to the victor and disadvantage to the vanquished.

These connections between war as the instrument of imperial *koinon* and the devastation of Earth were and are openly acknowledged and symbolically celebrated throughout the European history of conquest. Pliny the Elder described the parading in triumphal processions of a balsam-tree, representing Judea, as a statement that the land was now a subject of Rome and was paying tribute together with the race to which it had belonged.

> Numismatic and archaeological evidence similarly demonstrates Rome's rhetoric of conquest extending to the entire *oikumene*, to the ends of Earth. Statues and coins depict conquering emperors holding the orb or globe of the world in their hands. Beginning with Augustus, a series of coins depicted the emperor (*Caesar Divi*) standing triumphantly with his foot on the globe of the world. . . . Spectacular sculptures from a recently excavated imperial temple complex, the Sebasteoin, extend Rome's ideology of conquest explicitly to the whole Earth (*Ge*).[20]

Prior to that, Greece celebrated her successful colonization of the Galatians (Gauls) in the Great Frieze of Pergamon. In a detailed analysis of its mythic celebration of Greek triumphs over those they called "barbarians," Kahl pinpoints the fluid boundaries between mythological and historical enemies. Basic (in every sense) to confrontations between them is the confrontation between Athena, pitiless daughter of Zeus, at the top of the frieze, and Alkyoneus, youngest and favorite son of Ge/Gaia, the earth goddess. Gaia reaches up from the ground in a desperate plea for his life to be spared, and he remains invulnerable as long as he keeps contact with Gaia, the motherly ground. But Athena's leg comes between them and, as he is about to lose the life-preserving connection with the earth, the deadly poison of Athena's snake penetrates his chest.

> Directly above and unmoved by the tragedy of Gaia and her son, the winged goddess of victory, Nike, is approaching to adorn Athena with the crown of triumph.[21]

It is impossible here to do justice to the Frieze or to Kahl's detailed commentary on it. This brief reference simply serves to illustrate the larger point: that the imperial *koinon,* enforced through war on other peoples and on the earth that sustains all lives, is the direct mythic, cultural and religious opposite of the *koinonia* of the kingdom of God cultivated nonviolently by Jesus and central to the unity fostered by the apostles. Most important is the symbolic role played by God(s) in the action that determines and legitimizes which kind of unity is preferred and pursued. In the following chapters this distinction between the God of the *koinon* and the God of Jesus' *koinonia* will be discussed in relation to a vision of God implicit in a range of biblical narratives.

7

THE PRESENT-NESS OF THE KINGDOM

In the Gospel of Thomas, proper understanding
of the world and true self-recognition is made
possible through hearing Jesus' words of
wisdom. . . . There is no future or apocalyptic
notion of the Reign of God, such as one finds,
for example, in the synoptic gospels or in Paul.
Rather, what one finds is a concept of the Reign of
God whose chief characteristic is its present-ness
for those who are able correctly to perceive it.
—John S. Kloppenborg et al., *Q-Thomas Reader,* p. 99

The Christian identifier of *koinonia* was definitively established in the conversion of the gentile Cornelius. Or perhaps it would be more accurate to say that his conversion
established Peter's conversion to the practice of *koinonia*
and the revelation of a universal God. From that point on
he began to understand the implications of divine non-
discrimination, including the questions it raises about our
usual self-identification on the basis of race, creed, and
gender—or species.

The fundamental question is how we identify ourselves
in the sight of God; what Kloppenborg calls "our true self-
recognition made possible through hearing Jesus' words
of wisdom." To a large extent this has been done on the
basis of *who* we are as individuals in relation to our fellow
human beings. Peter first identified Cornelius as a gentile
rather than as another individual created by God. But even

this expansion of his vision would not have been enough. He began to learn that his God is universal, a God to whom *all* species are acceptable or "clean" by virtue of their goodness—that is, by being divinely created. That is the bedrock on which he personally was to cultivate unity from then on: by understanding that our Earth unity already exists and that its present-ness is called the kingdom of God.

This understanding of the present-ness of God identifies those who cultivate unity—even though they may not couch their understanding in such terms. They include Jesus and some of his followers as well as those who neither follow him nor understand his teachings, nor indeed have any knowledge of him. It is not doctrinal unity, but respecting diversity in all its forms and species that characterizes *koinonia*.

The 2010 Scholars Version of the Gospel of Thomas underlines this distinction between the Roman *koinon* and the *koinonia* of Jesus' vision by translating the Coptic term *tmntero* as "(*the Father's*) empire." Even though it does not always specify "of the Father," it is the most common predication for this term in Thomas. Like Peter's vision, in the following statement attributed to Jesus, this Gospel spells out the belief that *every* creature (except us?) knows that this empire is present *now* and *here* within our earthly situatedness:

> Jesus said, "If your leaders say to you, 'Look, the (Father's) empire is in the sky,' then the birds of the sky will precede you. If they say to you, 'It's in the sea,' then the fish will precede you. Rather, the (Father's) empire is inside you and outside you."[1]

These words concentrate the whole of existence within our shared earthly, concrete situation. We belong within God's empire by virtue of belonging within the community of life on earth that has evolved from a single organism in the oceans into all present life forms in and between sky, sea, and earth. This community of life continues to evolve as organisms sustain, perpetuate, and reproduce themselves. The chain of reference between ancestors and descendants, antecedents and consequents, is attested today not in doctrinal religious texts but by science, which identifies us as one species within the innovative, evolving chaos of life. This, says Jesus, is the father's empire: within us and outside us, here and now.

In the canonical Gospels, Jesus never calls for generic faith in "the kingdom" but always for trust in relation to something that can be immediately appropriated by us in thought or in action. The hearer is invited to follow Jesus into this vision of the world, and must decide while listening to his teaching whether she will be drawn into the world it invokes: that is, whether, like Peter, she will have faith and act on this vision or whether she will resist and withdraw.[2] Either way, this calls for an immediate decision about where the kingdom is, about what is involved in discovering it, and about what happens if and when it is discovered.

This is clearly stated near the end of the Gospel of Thomas:

> Jesus said, "The (Father's) empire is like a man who had a treasure in his field but didn't know it. And [when] he died, he left it to his [son]. The son [did] not know [about it either]. He took over the field and sold it. The buyer went plowing, discovered the treasure and began to lend money at interest to whomever he wished." (Thomas 109)

> His disciples said to him, "When will the (Father's) empire come?" [He replied] "It won't come by watching for it. It won't be said, 'Look, here!' or 'Look, there!' Rather, the Father's empire is spread out upon the earth, and people don't see it." (Thomas 113)

☙

In our literate age we are used to reading a text, weighing the pros and cons of the arguments proposed, and then making a decision about what it means for us. Such reflective responses built on association differ radically from the immediacy of oral transmission, for the latter is an *event* that draws us into what it involves. Reading texts, one focuses on the center, on what happens in the words, and can only hope that the structure and intention of the parable brings the "circumference"—that is, what is happening in the speaker and listener—into view.[3]

The *koinon* of doctrinal unity has meant that an "eventful" response is doubly difficult for those of us used to having the structure and intention of parables explained by someone presumed to have specialized knowledge of their content and context. These explanations are usually given in a formal religious setting, where those explaining them are presumed not only to have inside knowledge of their meaning, but also to know and believe in their putative message. Therefore the emphasis is on eliciting faith in that message, a faith that has too often focused on a kingdom in heaven and, by inference, not present on earth.

But in the Gospel of Thomas, Jesus' words leave us in no doubt that it is a kingdom open to and known by all earth's creatures; discoverable by us through consciously focusing on our shared relationships with God and learning from them. Jesus' parables do not elicit faith in a God in heaven, nor does the evangelist speak of Jesus' own faith. Jesus' word is not about faith; it *is* faith. It is faith in the double sense that it is spoken before God and gives expression to his own surrender to God in faith. But it does not ask us to believe in a particular sanctioned image of God. Nor does it take faith as its presupposition, but rather "godlessness". In fact, it sets a question mark against traditional human faith, asking whether it can, or perhaps must, be articulated in a language that is "godless."[4] Perhaps that of birds and fish?

Note that Job, when he justified himself rather than God as righteous, was told to look at God's ongoing relationship with the earth and its other-than-human living communities:

> Where were you when I laid the foundation of the earth?
> Tell me, if you have understanding . . .
> Or who shut the sea within its doors
> When it burst forth from the womb;
> When I made clouds its garment
> And thick darkness its swaddling band . . .
> Do you give the horse his might? . . .
> Is it by your wisdom that the hawk soars
> And spreads his wings toward the south?
> Is it at your command that the eagle mounts up
> And makes his nest on high? . . .
> Whatever is under the whole heaven is mine. . . . (Job 38:4–41:11)

Instead of hoping to enter that "whole" kingdom when we die, we are told that it is here, now, spread out upon the earth—but we do not see it. Jesus wrested the kingdom of God out of its customary mythic context where its meaning was taken for granted. Then he placed it in an alien context—alien, that is, to its mythological or accepted usage. Heard against this background, his parables clash with religious conventions. And they continue to do so, generating a new vision that grasps their referents in relation to a new conceptual field and a fresh contemporary experience of reality.[5]

Thus the "homeliness" of the parable of the leaven focuses attention on the role of women in creating the kingdom, that is, cultivating the conditions that unite ingredients so that an organism may develop rapidly. The version of this parable in the Gospel of Thomas is followed immediately by another that again puts a woman center stage, but in a very different light:

> The Father's empire is like [a] woman who took a little leaven, [hid] it in dough, and made it into large loaves of bread. Whoever has ears should listen. (Thomas 96)

> The (Father's) empire is like a woman who was carrying a [jar] full of meal. While she was walking along [a] distant road, the handle of the jar broke and the meal spilled behind her [along] the road. She didn't know it; she hadn't noticed a problem. When she reached her house, she put the jar down and discovered that it was empty. (Thomas 97)

As in the previous parable from the gospel of Thomas in which neither the owner of a field nor his son discover the treasure hidden there, she, too, is unaware that the treasure of the Father's empire is hidden in something as everyday as a field or its produce carried in a jar. And she fails to see that by cultivating an awareness of its presence and using its produce in routine ways, we play our part in the cultivation of the whole *koinonia* of that empire. Today, few religious conventions are shattered by Jesus' earthiness or by his parables. For these are now kept like empty jars, shelved in Christian commentaries, lexicons, and rituals, displayed and described in the context of doctrinal unity. They are presented as the very antithesis of godlessness and, owing more to imperially based and imposed legal systems than to Jesus' "godless" teaching, they lose their potential for shattering cultural and religious conventions.

This parabolic clash between *koinon* and *koinonia* was part of the religious inheritance of both Jesus and Peter. Yet both had to learn to trust a universal God who does not show partiality or discriminate:

> For the Lord your God is God of gods and Lord of lords,
> the great, the mighty, the terrible God, *who is not partial
> and takes no bribe*. (Deuteronomy 10:17, italics added)

As we have seen, Peter learnt this lesson in his encounter with Cornelius. Jesus learned it in his encounter with a Syro-Phoenician woman who asked him to heal her daughter of a demon. Jesus refused, using a symbolic image of "table-children-housedogs" to justify his decision. Jews considered dogs and swine unclean so they were used figuratively to characterize pagans, or gentiles. Accepting his imagery, she used it against him, reminding him that the goodness of God is abundant enough to satisfy not only the Jews but also the gentiles. The dogs, too, live by it—by eating the children's crumbs under the table (Mark 7:26–30). With this argument she exposed the partiality of his initial response and secured her daughter's—and gentiles'—liberation from the rhetoric of "unclean spirits" and ritual impurity. With that, she effectively caused a radical revision of Jesus' table fellowship.[6]

Jonah and the God of Jesus

This exemplary lesson about the total demand of *koinonia* within God's empire was anticipated in the Hebrew parable of Jonah. In fairness to Peter, who objected three times to being sent to convert Cornelius, he was not as recalcitrant as Jonah. As we saw, when the latter was told to bring a call for repentance to Nineveh, the archetypal godless empire, he fled in the opposite direction on a ship bound to Tarshish.

Yahweh responded, but in this case it was not with a cloth let down from heaven:

> YHWH now hurled a mighty wind upon the sea. A
> great gale churned the sea—the ship herself figured she

was about to break up. The sailors, terrified, shrieked each to his gods while they hurled the ship's cargo overboard hoping to diminish the threat hanging over them. Jonah, however, had gone below to the deepest hold where he now lay fast asleep. The skipper, coming upon him, cried: "What the blazes! Sound asleep? Up, up! Call to your gods. Maybe heaven will yet give us a thought . . . so that we shan't founder." The crew agreed to the suggestion: "Let's cast lots to discover on whose account this disaster has befallen us." They cast lots and the short one fell on Jonah. (Jonah 1:4–7)

The translator of this passage, Herbert Brichto, comments that the perplexing obtuseness of a prophet who undertakes flight from his God is underlined by his capacity for untroubled slumber while the ship heaves, crashes, and shudders in the hurricane's grip. In contrast to this, the increasingly desperate plight of ship and crew is reflected in the shipmaster's hope that calling on *their* gods might save them from foundering, and then by the crew's suggestion that they might cast lots in order to pinpoint the one responsible. For them, such misfortune was retribution for wrongdoing—by someone, sometime, somewhere.

They interrogate Jonah as to what he does, what brings him here and what land and people he belongs to. They assume that their passenger is vested with a high religious office. No minor functionary could draw upon himself such violent attention from so powerful a god. They endorse the mythic image of a God who exacts obedience from his subjects. Paradoxically, Jonah dismisses any such imputation by his actions and by identifying himself simply as an *"ibrí."* The term, says Brichto, stands for a person such as an indentured servant: in this case, a vassal, not of a mortal but of YHWH, "God of heaven, Creator of sea and land."[7]

The dramatic irony continues to build when the seamen assume that Jonah, a prophet privy to the will of the

Deity, will know the remedy for their plight. They ask and, sure enough, he gives them the answer: "Hurl me into the sea!" He doesn't offer to jump and they, pagans though they are, don't want to lay hands on such a sacred person. But their efforts to return to shore make no headway.

> Only then did they call upon YHWH: "Please, O YHWH, let us not perish in retribution for this man's life. Do not charge us with the murder of an innocent. You alone, YHWH, have willed all this!" With this they picked up Jonah and hurled him into the sea. Instantly the raging sea was calmed. (Jonah 1:14–15)

Previously the crew had called each to his own god. Now they address YHWH. In three terse sentences, says Brichto, they reveal theological good sense and moral scrupulousness that provide sardonic contrast to that of YHWH's prophet. Like Cornelius, they illustrate that the "godless" may be more receptive to God's word than those of traditional faith, such as Jonah.

Their previous refusal to save themselves at the cost of heaving Jonah overboard also shows a consideration for the preciousness of an individual life that will later appear in stark contrast to Jonah's own attitude. Also, their reluctance to save themselves at the cost of his life highlights his irresponsibility in fleeing from YHWH without regard for their safety.[8]

The text continues:

> YHWH commissioned a huge fish to swallow Jonah. Jonah spent three days and nights in the belly of that fish. Then Jonah prayed to God, YHWH, from the belly of that fish. (Jonah 2:1)

The psalm that follows does not appear anywhere else in the Bible. Brichto disagrees with modern scholars who say that it was borrowed from another context and interpolated by an anonymous editor. As the creation of the narrator himself, it makes excellent sense, for it continues the ironic contrast between the incongruous behavior of YHWH's chosen messenger and that of the pagan seamen. The voice from the belly of the fish acknowledges Jerusalem's shrine, the Temple, as the primary earthly terminal for a line of communication that stretches to YHWH's heavenly court.

But this is also, says Brichto, according to Judean theology, the only place on earth where sacrifice may be offered to YHWH. Jonah talks of offering sacrifice and paying vows in the Jerusalem Temple—all the while fleeing from his God! The seamen, however, offer sacrifice to YHWH immediately after the calming of the storm. The composition artfully contrives to bring into bold relief the absurdity of the prophet's plight and contrasts his behavior with that of the pagan seamen. Similarly Cornelius, though terrified by his vision, does what he is told, whereas Peter argues with God on the grounds of his observance of God's law (Acts 10:14–16).

Jonah's psalm marks the hinge in the drama's action, says Brichto—the point of change or reversal. But as he resumes his journey toward Nineveh, we see him unchanged in heart or spirit. The fish, however, obeyed YHWH's command and "spat Jonah out onto the shore." Once again he is commanded to go to Nineveh, that great city, and deliver his proclamation:

> "Forty days more and Nineveh will lie in ruins!" The magistrates of Nineveh, believing in heaven, proclaimed a fast; sackcloth was worn by great and small alike. The king left his throne, threw off his royal robe, donned sackcloth and sat in ashes. His heralds cried throughout Nineveh, "By the decree of the king and his councilors: Neither humans and cattle, herds and flocks, not a one is to taste anything, nor feed; not a nibble of grass nor a sip of water. All are to don sackcloth—humans and cattle alike—all are to call upon heaven with might and main! Each and all are to turn back from evildoing or

any lawlessness they are engaged in. Who knows but
that heaven will turn around and relent of its purpose,
turn back from fury's course—and we not perish?"

God took notice of their doings, of their turnabout
from their wicked ways. So God, relenting of the punishment he had threatened upon them, did nothing.
(Jonah 3:4–10)

In its heyday Nineveh was a huge city covering some
eighteen thousand acres. The capital of the world's greatest pagan empire, it boasted a population of 120,000. Yet
it now accepts the indictment of an alien prophet from a
small and distant hill town, and this without the perfor-
mance of a single sign or wonder to support the judgment
and threat he proclaims. More remarkable still, guilt is
admitted on the very first day of the prophet's call and repentance is immediate, total and absolute. Jonah's survival
in the fish's belly for three days pales by comparison with
this extraordinary human behavior.

And this behavior—a pagan city brought to instanta-
neous acceptance of and obedience to God's word—stands
in antithetic parallel to the prophet's rejection of God's
command at the beginning of the narrative. On the one
hand, an entire population accepts one man's voice as representing that of the Deity; while on the other, that man
rejects the divine voice that speaks directly to him.[9] This
antithesis is echoed in the Samaritan woman's call for her
countrymen to accept a Jew, Jesus, as a prophet. And we are
told that although many of them did (John 4:29), his own
people rejected him (John 1:1).

An even more extraordinary feature of the Jonah parable stresses the "earthiness" of God's empire—that is,
the divine impartiality that embraces other-than-human
species. Furthermore, the prophet's decree is accepted and
acted upon by the people of Nineveh as applying to human and cattle alike. The animals, too, are to fast and wear

sackcloth, and all are to invoke God so that by their com-
pliance all may escape from punishment. This acceptance
of the collective nature of punishment and forgiveness
was also evident in Hosea's mission to the people of Judah
and Israel referred to earlier. He had found no faithfulness,
kindness, or knowledge of God in the land. Instead there
was lying, killing, stealing, adultery, and murder following
murder. Meanwhile, he says, the land mourns and all who
dwell in it languish, as do the beasts of the field and the
birds of the air. Even the fish are swept from the sea (Hosea
4:1–3).

Reading Jonah or Hosea today, one is struck by the
prescience of their authors, by their pre-scientific understanding of the interconnectedness of all species and of the
effects of human behavior on all living beings—for good
or ill. But the prophets differ in their response to this state
of affairs. In Hosea's case, those who repent, who return to
the Lord, "shall flourish as a garden, blossom as a vine and
their fragrance shall be like the wine of Lebanon" (Hosea
14:7). In other words, he is hopeful that they will respond
to his call for repentance and is happy to envisage its effects.

How does Jonah react?

> Jonah was terribly displeased and angry. He prayed
> to YHWH: "Now then, was this not what I predicted
> back in my native land? My reason for taking flight to
> Tarshish? How well I know that you are a gracious and
> compassionate God, slow to anger, abounding in stead-
> fast love and relenting when it comes to punishment!
> So now, YHWH, take my life—I would far rather die
> than live." YHWH said, "My, you really are upset, aren't
> you!" (Jonah 4:1–4)

Why is Jonah so disgruntled? His complaint is that
YHWH gave him a message to deliver but did not necessarily intend to carry it out. He hoped to save rather than
destroy Nineveh and its inhabitants! The implication is

that Jonah knew this and that's why he went to Tarsish. For Jonah, in God's place, would not have accepted their repentance. His complaint is not with the response of the Ninevites but with God's response to their response. God's attributes of patience, pity, and compassion would inevitably result (as indeed happened) in the sparing of Nineveh, and the reluctant prophet's prediction would prove false. Think of the shame he would suffer!

The clear implication, says Brichto, is that Jonah knew from the start that his God is, in colloquial terms, a pushover. The divine attribute of forgiveness causes him to despair. He'd rather die than carry on serving such a God. God's response to this is, says Brichto, as sardonic as it is terse. We should also note, he says, the absurdity of a prophet's being reduced to despair by the success of his mission.[10]

These reversals of expectation in regard to God are an all-important feature of parable in the Bible. The God whose Temple is in Jerusalem is seen to have mercy on Ninevite, Samaritan, Jew and gentile alike—and on their birds, beasts and fish. They are treated as one by God, both in sin and in repentance. Yet within the lifetimes of Jonah and of Jesus the dominant religious images of the kingdom of God were those of power, dominion, and sovereignty associated with royal and imperial households. These images pervade the so-called "Royal Psalms" (2, 20, 21, 45, 72, 101, 110, 132):

> He who sits in the heavens laughs;
> The Lord has them in derision.
> Then he will speak to them in his wrath,
> And terrify them in his fury, saying,
> "I have set my king
> on Zion, my holy hill. . . ."
> Now therefore, O kings, be wise;
> Be warned, O rulers of the earth.

> Serve the Lord with fear,
> With trembling kiss his feet,
> Lest he be angry, and you perish in the way. (Psalm 2:4–6, 10–11)

Such biblical expectations of how God acts, of where the Kingdom of God is found, and how God is to be served were clearly shared by Jonah. Indeed, he held them so strongly that he found it impossible to accept the image of a forgiving, nondiscriminatory God. At the same time, says Brichto, he knew in his heart that if the Ninevites responded properly to his message, God would forgive them. Parable exposes such "double-think": if we weren't prone to it there would be no eventful upsetting of our routine expectations. In that context, a contrary image forestalls thought; its vividness or strangeness leaves us doubtful about how to monitor or rationalize our reaction.

Jesus asks those who hear or recite Psalms such as those above to see the Kingdom of God in the yeast a woman uses to make bread. Yeast, a woman and some flour. Is that all it takes to create God's kingdom? Our suspended disbelief means that the parable does not finish until we, the listeners, are drawn into it as participants by being forced to ask such questions of ourselves.[11] Or, in Jonah's case, half-drowned and then dragged into asking them.

What happens when he does? He refuses to change his mind. Disgruntlement is a poor word to describe his emotional state. He'd rather die than change his mind and live. He'd rather die than change his image of God and live. God's sardonic answer is to a child in a tantrum. It underlines the irony of a prophet taking the "conversion" of his audience *in response to his warning* as a sign of his failure.[12]

So he goes out of the city, sits down under an improvised lean-to and waits to see what will happen in the city. Then:

YHWH commissioned a broad-leafed vine to climb over Jonah's lean-to and serve him as a shade and provide relief from his misery. Jonah was ecstatic. God commissioned a worm-pest at daybreak to attack the vine so that it shriveled. Then at sunrise God commissioned an east wind of numbing effect. The sun beat down on Jonah's head; he languished so that he told himself to give up the ghost: "Better death than to live so." God said to Jonah, "Upset, are you?—on the vine's account?" He answered, "Grievously upset—I long for death." YHWH then said, "You have been brought to such concern for the vine, over which you exerted no labor, in whose growth you played no part, which in the space of a night came to be and in the space of a night perished. And I—I am to show no concern for Nineveh, this great city, within which there is a human populace of twelve times ten thousand humans and more who cannot tell right hand from left—to say nothing of cattle?" (Jonah 4:6–11)

Jonah's grief—if that's the right word—is not for the plant but for himself. God's response contrasts the infinite dimensions of divine concern with the self-centered interests of the prophet who claims to be God's instrument. And, God satirically suggests, if Jonah has no feeling for humanity, perhaps he cares about the cattle? Just as the Syro-Phoenician woman assumes that God cares about the dogs. Brichto does not see the central message of the text in Jonah's finding fault with God's exercise of compassion that foreordained (as he sees it) the failure of his mission. Nor in the absurdities of a prophet seeking to evade his calling, an unprecedentedly immediate and absurd conversion to repentance of an entire populace, and in the prophet's despair over the success of his mission.

Rather, as I have done with Jesus, Peter, and Cornelius, Brichto focuses on the fact that Nineveh was a non-Israelite city, the capital of the Assyrian Empire that had destroyed the Northern kingdom, Israel. This set the pattern for its neo-Babylonian successors who destroyed the Southern kingdom, Judah, and put YHWH's Jerusalem Temple to the torch. For the Jews, this resulted in a xenophobic hatred for all non-Jewish peoples, and by extension their flocks and herds. The book of Jonah, says Brichto, is a protest against this prevailing mood.

> Jonah is a symbol of the Jewish people, chosen as God's prophet-people to the nations, which is now being chastised for its unbecoming hatred for the gentiles and called back to *its true vocation as a prophetic witness to God's love for all humanity*, including those who had smitten it on both cheeks. There is nothing inherently implausible in a single prophet standing, in a parable, for collective Israel.[13] (italics added)

There are clear parallels here with the parabolic stories of Jesus, Peter and Cornelius, even though the plot in Acts is significantly removed from the situation in Jonah and all are yet further displaced from the lives of those reading them today. So the characters do not lure us into self-identification. But if they are understood within the mythic framework of the Bible itself, as of course they must be, then we, too, are left with God's final question to Jonah ringing in our ears:

> And I—am I to show no concern for Nineveh, this great city, with which there is a human populace of twelve times ten thousand humans and more who cannot tell right hand from left—to say nothing of cattle? (Jonah 4:11)

8

BIODIVERSITY AND GOD

If the Bible were only about peace through victory, we would not need it. If it were only about peace through justice, we would not believe it.
—John Dominic Crossan, *God and Empire*, p. 94

God's rebuke to Jonah for ignoring the universal reach of divine concern is echoed in the sharp rebuke to Peter: "Stop designating 'unclean' what God has made pure!" (Acts 10:15). Both reproofs call on us to reject religiously validated ideas of God that sanction religious taboos and violence against all creatures, both human and other-than-human. But since the rejection comes from the same God in whose name the taboos and violence are invoked, this conflict *within the Bible itself* between visions of God forces us, says Crossan, to decide between them.

For Peter, that decisive moment comes when his religious exclusivism is exposed by setting it against God's inclusive love for all species: all creatures are "good" by virtue of, literally, being created "good." This expands the range and scope of Jesus' saying that the only valid point of comparison for our relationships with others is that of God's relationship with them—irrespective of whether we deem them good or bad, just or unjust, friend or enemy. As James Robinson points out:

> The term "Son of God" occurs in Q, but there it is not introduced as a Christological title but rather as a name for all the disciples of Jesus who, like God, cared even

for their enemies. "Love your enemies and pray for those persecuting you, so that you may become sons of your Father, for he raises his sun on bad and good and rains on the just and unjust." (Q 6:22–23)[1]

Therefore, if we are to be like the Father, it means cultivating the unity of the Father's empire and, like Jesus, returning love for hatred and nonviolence for violence. Being a son or daughter of God means having and making no enemies, refusing to react violently to others on the basis of their religious, racial, or social status. A "war of all against all" is out of the question,

> [f]or in Christ Jesus you are all sons of God, through faith. For as many of you as were baptized into Christ have put on Christ. There is neither Jew nor Greek, there is neither slave nor free, there is neither male nor female; for you are all one in Christ Jesus. (Galatians 3:26–28)

On a symbolic level this means that both circumcised Jews and uncircumcised Galatians stand under the authority of Israel's God alone. This, says Brigitte Kahl, smashes an icon of Roman law and order, and with it all previous boundaries between us based on race, religion, class, and gender. On a symbolic level it is a withdrawal from previous participation in the *koinon* of imperial religion, and as such probably represents the actual storm centre of the Galatian correspondence.[2]

∽

Today, however, when a political consensus supports the need for and gradual implementation of laws against discrimination against our fellow human beings on the bases of race, religion, class, and gender, it is Peter's conversion that makes an even greater demand on our inclusivity. Its point of reference is not simply our discriminating against each other on these anachronistic grounds, but the creation of *all* species by God. This places them within the remit of God's love and therefore of ours too. Our concern for the well-being of our own species is to be based on God's ongoing creative relationships with all other species as well. At the very least, the unity of God's love for all requires of us a desire to respect the integrity of all and so to foster our common well-being. As Jonah and Peter came to recognize, however reluctantly, God's indiscriminate love for *all* living beings is the benchmark for our conduct toward those of our own species.

Such a reversal of priorities in our perception of the nature of our relationships is as difficult for us as it was for Jonah and Peter, especially in a highly individualistic cultural and religious climate. But in the United Nations Decade on Biodiversity and with the Declaration of 2010 as the International Year of Biodiversity, there is a concerted effort to broaden our view of the nature of biodiversity and the role it plays in our lives. Diversity of species is acknowledged as having an essential role in sustaining our capacity for life and, therefore, for all types of relationships with others. Its significance within our physical environments and the planetary ecosystem is unquestionable, no matter how aware or unaware of it we may be, and whether or not we experience it as individuals.

At stake here is a leap of faith—practical, political and scientific—that opens us to an earthly as well as religious reality. As we exist within it as part of a greater whole, we can never fully grasp its mystery nor successfully analyze it. But since we do exist within it, so, too, are we loved by the God who creates the whole.

Jesus understood this and characterized the effects of what to us is the shocking *mode* of God's love: it is poured out on the just and the unjust alike. While acknowledging that there are those whom we may (rightly) deem our enemies and persecutors, the model for our conduct toward them is that of a God who causes the sun to shine indiscriminately on those we categorize as friend or enemy. So, too, the rain falls on and sustains the lives of *all* earthly beings, including those species and creatures whose existence we are unaware of as well as those we routinely ignore.

From these undeniable facts emerges an overarching view of God as both exemplar and arbiter of the nature of our relationships with all other creatures. While Jesus acknowledges that human relationships may be shaped not by love, but by hatred and persecution, he does not accept that this is the proper religious basis on which to build them. And from what we know of his life and the manner of his death, he exemplifies that all-embracing love within a society that, as Jonah and Peter demonstrate, held religiously, implicitly and explicitly, to the model of an all-powerful, vengeful and therefore violent God. By identifying God as the precise antithesis of this in his sayings, his actions, and the manner of his life and death, Jesus himself becomes a parable of God.

Indeed, this is how many of the prophetic elements of the Bible present God to us—implicitly in the case of Jonah, explicitly in that of Peter, and demonstrably in the life of Jesus. But both Jonah and Peter saw the real creatures before them, those alive and present in the natural world, as other than those that God had declared "good." Therefore, the God they invoked to support their prejudices was neither (as Peter came to understand) the God of the Genesis narrative nor the impartial God of Deuteronomy. Nor did such a Deity support Jonah's view of the cattle of Nineveh. He could not envisage them being receptive to God's collective call to repentance and thus worthy of the "goodness" that was theirs according to their kind. As Paul Waldau points out, the prevailing religious assumption is that the lives of these creatures, although connected in some way to the phenomenon of life in the human species, are at best not only different from ours but also of little or no comparative value in the eyes of God.[3]

๛

This assumption was and is too easily taken as an implicit divine license to discriminate against them and use them as we will. Worse yet, this attitude is explicitly attributed to God in the Bible and enshrined in a later Genesis narrative:

> And God blessed Noah and his sons, and said to them, "Be fruitful and multiply and fill the earth. The fear of you and the dread of you shall be upon every beast of the earth, and upon every bird of the air, upon everything that creeps upon the ground and all the fish of the sea; into your hand they are delivered." (Genesis 9:2–3)

To some extent, this both explains and reinforces the shock felt by Jonah and Peter when rebuked by God on the grounds of the goodness of every beast, reptile, fish, and bird. It also drives home the complex nature of our relationships with other species as recorded in the biblical texts—and of the texts themselves.

> But ask the beasts, and they will teach you;
> The birds of the air, and they will tell you;
> Or the plants of the earth, and they will teach you;
> And the fish of the sea will declare to you.
> Who among all these does not know that
> The hand of the Lord has done this?
> In God's hand is the life of every living thing
> And the breath of all humankind. (Job 12:7–10)

Metaphorical and other figurative statements in the Bible about nonhuman animals are routinely used either to denigrate (as in the encounter between Jesus and the Syro-Phoenician woman) or to elevate them in God's eyes (as in the above passage from Job). And so they were and are subsequently employed to justify human attitudes toward them:

> The Bible contains, in fact, two models for thinking
> about humans and animals: one paradisal, the other
> this-worldly and realistic. The first way uses the picture
> of peace with and between wild animals as a metaphor
> for cosmic and social peace; the second way sees peace
> from them as a practical aspect of desired shalom.[4]

Of these two pictures, the implicitly violent second one
dominates the outlook represented by Jonah and to a
lesser extent, by Peter. Both stories reflect the influence
of a *koinon* of imperial power that routinely used human
violence to overpower and subdue other peoples and with
them, Gaia/Earth and her other-than-human offspring.
The latter's "captivity" was taken for granted as a profit-
able by-product of the conquest of other people and their
lands. The physical fertility of those lands and the animals
inhabiting them, insofar as it contributed to the imperial
coffers, was all that mattered. This explains, though it does
not excuse, Jonah's conduct and his unrepentant response
to Yahweh. As Brichto points out, he saw Nineveh as the
capital of the Assyrian empire, which long before the
Roman conquest had destroyed the Northern Kingdom,
Israel. This set the pattern for its neo-Babylonian successors
who destroyed the Southern Kingdom, Judah, deported its
inhabitants, and put the Jerusalem Temple of YHWH to
the torch.[5]

Both Jonah and Peter reflect the biblical tension between identifying God, first, with a paradisal, nonviolent,
and therefore unrealistically idealist view of peace between
all species, and second, with a reductionist realism that
confirms an adversarial view of our relationships with
them. If the latter, then God condones our destruction of
their bodies, their habitats, and even their species in the
blind pursuit of our human interests. It is such a concept
of God that filled the coffers of Nineveh, Babylon, and

Rome—and continues to fill those of the world's biggest banks and corporations today.

֍

The pivotal question, then and now, is whether God is identified as being concerned with the welfare of all creatures—or only of us human beings. Implicit in this question and evident in answers to it is the difference between two modes of power attributed to God. Crossan defines them by distinguishing between them:

> I always find power ambiguous until it becomes clear whether we are dealing with the violent power of domination or the nonviolent power of persuasion.[6]

How can we relate these two modes of exercising power to God? In the violent mode the emphasis is on notional and physical separation between us and other creatures and between them and God. The nonviolent mode moves us decisively toward connection with them; indeed it relies on and fosters a sense of being connected to others, whether through religion, race, gender, interdependence, or common genetic and earthly origins and lives. By doing so, it also moves us decisively toward identifying God with nonviolent power.

Of course, this is not always clear-cut. To Jonah, God's power may have appeared violent rather than persuasive. After all, he was half-drowned and then swallowed by a huge fish! And he reacted accordingly. But in the final picture of the relationship between God and his prophet we discern divine forbearance in a final attempt at persuading him to see God's essential inclusiveness. We are left to decide for ourselves whether or not it succeeds. God's overarching pity toward all creatures may or may not finally have persuaded Jonah to feel the same way toward the pagan Ninevites, their animals and their plants.

As the opposite of coercion, persuasion leaves us free to change our minds—or not. Peter too had to be persuaded to feel differently about other creatures—and almost incidentally, about gentile human beings also. The persuasion was based on an appeal to the common origin of all created beings and the "goodness" this confers on all alike. A proper response to this appeal requires a conversion to the relevant point of view and would be a long process. Peter said, "I am *beginning* to understand that our God does not discriminate" (Acts 10:34). But this was his crucial first move toward *koinonia* on an ever-expanding scale characterized as understanding what it means to belong within what Jesus terms "my Father's empire."

Today, scientific research offers us a similar kind of persuasion by demonstrating the cosmic, earthly and physiological degree of our connectedness and interdependence. Its evidence for this ranges from the common planetary origins of all earthly life and the shared biological features of our bodies to our mutual dependence on other species for survival within the global environment and on its ability to sustain the conditions favorable for life to exist. This may or may not persuade us to live out of an ever-deepening sense of connectedness between ourselves and other creatures. For some Christians that may be strengthened by the religious belief in our common creation by God and the declaration that in God's eyes, if not in ours, the whole of creation, ourselves included, is "good." Other Christians, however, follow Noah's example and believe they are licensed to use other creatures violently.

For us too, as for Jonah and Peter, the cultural challenge is whether or not we identify ourselves as being continually sustained by and dependent on the diverse community of life on earth. That in turn influences our response to the religious challenge: do we see God as having a special or even an exclusive concern for us as members of that community, or, does her concern extend to all of us equally and to our interactions? Wisdom (in all her forms) has no doubt about their exemplary role:

> Go to the ant, o sluggard;
> Consider her ways and be wise.
> Without having any chief, officer or ruler,
> She prepares her food in summer,
> And gathers her sustenance in harvest. (Proverbs 6:6–8)

Yet Jesus draws quite a different moral from the natural world:

> Look at the birds of the air; they neither sow nor reap nor gather into barns, and yet your heavenly Father feeds them. . . .
> Consider the lilies of the field, how they grow; they neither toil nor spin;
> Yet I tell you, even Solomon in all his glory was not arrayed like one of these. (Matthew 6:26, 28)

Do we use one rather than the other image to legitimate either a sense of connectedness to or of separation from the lives of other members of the Earth community? If we choose one that endorses a sense of separation, then our actions and their potentially violent character may appear to be endorsed by God.

This means that, like Jonah, we may decide whether or not all actions we attribute to God are to be identified by force and violence or by persuasion and attraction:

> For the Bible forces us to witness the struggle of these two transcendental visions within its own pages and to ask ourselves how we decide between them. It presents us with the radicality of a just and nonviolent God repeatedly and relentlessly confronting the normalcy of an unjust and violent civilization.[7]

At stake now for us in this scientific *and* religious quandary is what Crossan calls "the land-as-life": land that in the Torah is the material basis of life itself. Land-as-life is a microcosm of earth-as-life, because according to the Psalms "the earth is the Lord's and all that is in it; the world, and those who live in it" (Psalm 24:1).[8] It is depressingly true to say that today, outside of very small enclaves, a perilously "normal" civilization triumphs over the radicality of a just and nonviolent God. But again, as both Waldau and Crossan make clear, this can be and too often is "justified" because of the ambiguity attached to divine power in the biblical records.

In spite of, or perhaps because of, this ambiguity, the crowning glory of biblical distributive justice lies in a reversal of the dispossession of land, people (slaves), and animals—a pattern formulated in the sequential laws from Sabbath Day to Sabbath Year to Sabbath Jubilee—that sought to liberate people from debt obligation and debt enslavement (Leviticus 25:10). Then and now this is God's demand for a just distribution of land-as-life, a practical *koinonia* based on the goodness of all creatures in the creation theology of Genesis. But does it—or can it—wield any persuasive power in today's world? If not, the victory over God's radicality is won by those who have held and still hold unswervingly to violent power exercised over land-as-life: all too often in God's name. This imperialist *koinon* has characterized Christian colonial power throughout history.

9

JESUS TESTED BY GOD

One cannot divide one's life between an
actual relationship to God and an inactual I–It
relationship to the world—praying to God in
truth and utilizing the world. Whoever knows
the world as something to be utilized knows
God the same way.
—Martin Buber, *I And Thou*, p. 156

Just as Jonah and Peter were tested on their understanding
of God and the nature of divine and imperial power, so,
too, was Jesus. Like Job, he was tested on God's behalf by
the devil, otherwise known as Satan, who in the Hebrew
Bible is a member of God's heavenly court, and not an embodiment of evil (Job 1:1; Zechariah 3:1–2).

> And Jesus was guided into the wilderness by the Spirit
> to be put to the test by the devil. (Q 4:1–2; Matthew
> 4:1–11; Luke 4:1–13)

> And he was with wild beasts. (Mark 1:13)

The contextual setting for his test, "the wilderness," has
allowed commentators to enlarge on a theme previously
mentioned—the opposing attitudes to "wilderness" and
"wild beasts," that envision them either as paradisal or as
a focus for conflict between good and evil. "Wilderness"
also resonates with *the voice of one crying in the wilderness*
(cf. Isaiah 40:3), linking it to Israel's escape route when
fleeing from Pharaoh's Egyptian Empire. This enabled Jews
to see it as a place for new acts of liberation from imperial

power that would echo those of old and restore right relationships within Israel. Recalling their Exodus experiences, they could also regard wilderness as a sanctuary from sinful society and a place to draw near to God. An overtone of that appears in Mark 1:13, where angels minister to Jesus.

The tension between all these competing senses of connection and separation must be borne in mind while remembering that the ancient Hebrews had ample reason to regard the wilderness as cursed because of its forbidding character and lack of water. From that perspective, the wilderness was an inhuman space, the domain of wild animals and inimical to humans. Even today we often attach these negative associations to the other-than-human inhabitants of areas not dominated by us.[1]

Whichever aspect of wilderness we concentrate on, however, it discloses an inherent problem. Whatever happened to Jesus during his solitary ordeal or Jonah in the fish's belly, there is no witness to testify to it. The dialogue between Jesus and the devil cannot be verified. We are simply told about this mythic "relational event" in which the Spirit that drove Jesus into the desert was, like the air in which he breathed, between him and God.[2]

Nevertheless, within the mythic continuum of describing encounters between humans and God, it gives a coherent account of a collective ethos and a religious worldview that resonates with the prophetic critique of abuses of earthly power carried out in God's name. The narrative centers on three specific tests, each revelatory of some fundamental aspect of Jesus' vision of God and of his relationship with the kingdom of God on Earth. These emerge as answers to questions put to him by the devil and in various ways reflect attempts by his disciples (then and now) to understand that vision and relationship. Did he, for example, consider himself a "son of God," and if so, what kind of God? A serviceable, useful one who can save him and others from hunger and danger and give him power over all the Earth?

The First Test

> And he ate nothing for forty days, and he became hungry, and the devil told him, "If you are God's Son, order that these stones become loaves."
>
> And Jesus answered him, "It is written: *a person is not to live only by bread but on every word that comes from God's mouth.*" (Matthew 4:2–4)

Jesus' answer reveals an understanding and acceptance of what it means to be human. It means reconciling one's bodily needs and desires with the way in which, as a believing Jew, he has learnt to understand God's relationship with him and with the Earth. He accepts that the conditions for human existence have developed naturally since the time when "all things began": fasting makes us hungry and hunger is relieved by bread; but stones cannot instantly become bread. On that basis, Jesus responds to this test, as to those that follow, with a quotation from the Septuagint version of Deuteronomy: *It is written: a person is not to live only by bread but by every word that comes from God's mouth* (Deuteronomy 8:3).

This reinforces the case for a narrator other than Jesus, since he would almost certainly have quoted a Hebrew or Aramaic version of the Scriptures. But whatever the version, it reflects the thinking of a first-century Palestinian Jew. This enabled Christians to refute claims that Jesus was inspired by someone other than the God of Moses. Within the Mosaic tradition the test-response narrative used in the cases of Jonah, Job, and Peter challenges both contemporary and later presuppositions about the power we assume to be granted us by God or exercised by God on our behalf. Within a *koinon*, that power is seized and exercised ruthlessly in war and conquest and assumes physical, political, and commercial mastery over all the inhabitants of Earth, human and nonhuman alike, and also over all natural resources. This is what Buber characterizes as an "I–It" relationship with God and with the world.

Jesus rejects that vision of a "God of the gaps," one who can be "used" to compensate for our weaknesses and inadequacies. Changing stones into bread might satisfy his hunger. But it would also require belief in a God ready to impose his will on the natural order on Jesus' behalf. That would indeed provide all who heard (or read) of the event with proof of his unique status and power within the Father's empire. But within this empire the Father does not exercise that kind of utilitarian power. The same passage in Deuteronomy that acknowledges Jesus' need for food also asserts the necessity of living by the logic and grace of God's universal love in a *koinonia* that respects all living beings. So while our power and the might of our hands might get us all the material things we desire, we do not live only by them. As with the Israelites in the wilderness, Jesus' ordeal by hunger happened *"so that God might know what was in their hearts and whether or not they would keep his commandments"* (Deuteronomy 8:2f.).

This reminds us of something we know perfectly well but too often forget: that while we need God-given manna and bread, they alone cannot sustain us (Deuteronomy 8:3). Material things satisfy our bodily needs. But, says the Deuteronomist, when we have eaten and are full, have good houses and live in them, when our herds and flocks, gold and silver, stocks and shares multiply, beware! For we may then be tempted to say, *"**My** power and the might of **my** hand have got me this wealth"* (Deuteronomy 8:12–18). In fact, of course, our power as individuals is always dependent on the ability of the whole community of life on earth to sustain us.

But the devil's appeal to Jesus to use God's power has an even deeper purpose. It would prove (to the devil or to the evangelist?) whether or not he is indeed God's Son. Two of the tempter's three tests are focused on defining and defending the use of that title. Jesus rejects the implication that he might utilize that relationship with God for his own comfort and safety. Instead he validates his true status as one who knows, observes, and conforms to its true meaning: to know and observe Torah faithfully (Deuteronomy 8:3; 6:13, 16).

But what leads the devil (evangelist?) to ask the question, that is, to entertain the possibility that Jesus *is* the Son of God? James Robinson poses and answers that question by pointing out that if there were no baptismal scene in Mark 1: 9–11, with the voice from heaven announcing, "You are my Son, the Beloved," then putting the title in question would be unnecessary.[3]

Instead, undergoing the test would prove that it was *God* who could, so to speak, be put to the test—or rather that God could be used to establish our true place and role in the world. The whole notion here of testing the nature of God prepares us for the definitive answer given later by Jesus to the question of what makes any of us, including him, "children of God":

> Love your enemies and pray for those persecuting you,
> so that you may become sons of your Father; for he
> raises his sun on the bad and good and rains on the just
> and unjust. (Q 6:22–23)

To love one's enemies rather than to fight and kill them means accepting that they, too, belong within the Father's *koinonia*, where the sun and rain do not discriminate between friend and enemy, but warm and nourish all alike. Those we call bad or good, just or unjust, share the gifts of sun, rain, and land with us. Understanding and living by this gift relationship between us and Earth means not reducing it to a purely utilitarian one that is seen to serve our interests alone.[4] If that is the only way we know the world, then we know others—and indeed God—in the same way. But if our relationship to God is actually one based on love, forgiveness, and respect, then the world "becomes wholly present" to us.[5] This is what makes each of us a son or daughter of God. In practice it means turning the other cheek, giving the shirt off one's back, going the second mile, lending without ever asking for anything in return.[6]

Living in such a relationship with the God of *koinonia* is the polar opposite of accepted practice within an imperial *koinon* that defines itself, its land, and its members by separation from those outside it—and by its ability to destroy its enemies through military force and appropriate their lands. Echoing Buber's insight of the world becoming "wholly present" to us, Gregory Bateson uses the word "sacred" to describe that condition of wholeness. Sacredness is that which binds the whole together. Attempts to utilize it by unbinding it (by force, by war) or dissecting it in order to manipulate it (by turning stones into bread) assume that it is external to our existence. Yet, throughout human history we—or at least the sages among us—have somehow been able to intuit that sacred unity within which we belong and to whose cultivation we desire to commit ourselves. But precisely because of its wholeness, we have never been able to define it by anything other than itself.[7]

This insight into the reality of our lives, couched here in religious terms, strikes a particular chord in a time of climate change. We have long known in theory but are now learning the hard way that we are not only free to cultivate "the whole" or not, but that we also depend absolutely on it—on everything at once that proceeds "out of the mouth of God": that is, from the earth, sun, skies, and waters together. Earth as a whole has the power to generate life in the soil and in the waters and to nourish diverse living beings; power over time to turn invisible elements as well as stone, clay, or soil into edible crops—and back again into stone. It is not we who possess these powers. Just the reverse. We have demonstrated our power to turn cropland into a "Dust Bowl" through overproduction, chemical pollution, and contamination of water resources. Our economies are built on the presupposition that as individuals we can, and indeed should turn bread into gold and silver by speculating on future market prices and storing the profit in bank vaults. These returns have now become truly and properly invisible, appearing as virtual realities on global stock exchanges. They generate no new life and nourish no life-form.

This is where the dual aspects of climatic change, of thinking about the scientific/cultural as well as the religious climate, merge into one. We have inherited religious teachings that consistently devalue or at best ignore the earthly resources that sustain all lives and life-forms in favor of gaining a treasure in heaven routinely referred to and accepted as our "salvation"—and implicitly ours alone. This religious form of apartheid stands exposed by Pythes' wife who, despite living within an imperial *koinon*, understood and dealt with the real and present effects of her husband's self-regarding disregard of the well-fare and well-being of the community as a whole. True, we do not live by bread alone. But neither can we live without it or any other of Earth's gifts—and their givers.

The Second Test of Jesus' Vision

If we use financial, military, technological or religious power to assert a notional independence from our bodily needs, then we fail the first test. An acceptance of the nature of our human dependence can be seen in the reality of

Jesus' hunger after a long fast, in his retort that we do not live by bread alone, and in his decision to accept hunger rather than invoke extra-earthly power to relieve it. Each of us, he suggests, has enough independence to make decisions about how we deal with our dependence on others. And in this second test he similarly affirms the delicate balance between his own physical limitations in regard to Earth's gravitational pull and the overriding gravity of his relationship with God. The formal conditions of his existence, created by God, can never be cast aside in order to demonstrate that he exists solely by virtue of that creative power:

> Then the devil conducts him to the holy city, sets him on the high point of the temple and says to him, "To prove you're God's son, jump off; remember, it is written,
> *To his heavenly messengers he will give orders about you,*
> *and with their hands they will catch you,*
> *so you won't even stub your toe on a stone."*
> Jesus said to him, "Elsewhere it is written,
> *You shall not put the Lord your God to the test."* (Matthew 4:5–7)

This test was a variation on the first and also involves a change of scene. The devil takes Jesus to Jerusalem and sets him on the pinnacle of the temple. But once again the challenge is to prove that he is God's son—this time by defying the laws of gravity that keep him, like all of us, bound to earth. If he is God's son he should (supposedly) be able to jump from the pinnacle of the temple and remain unhurt, for angels would bear him up and he would be unharmed (Psalm 91:11–12).

The move from the wilderness to Jerusalem is a powerful reminder of the archetypal journey of the Jews from Egypt and their wanderings in the wilderness of Sin between Elim and Sinai (Exodus 16:1; 17:1). Jesus' refusal to jump because this would "test God" refers directly to the Exodus account of the time in the wilderness when the Israelites were thirsty and found fault with Moses because there was no water to drink. Moses said that by doing so they "put God to the test." But when they complained that they had been brought out of Egypt only to be killed by thirst, God told Moses to strike the rock at Horeb and from it came water for them to drink. Moses called this place Massah, translated as *test* or *proof*, because there they had "put God to the test" (Exodus 17:1–7).

But *when they are brought into the land*, they must test God no further, but "do what is right and good in the sight of the Lord . . . that he might preserve us alive, as at this day" (Deuteronomy 6:16–25). Jesus quotes this text, using his ancestors' wilderness experience to drive home the lesson that to do what the devil asks would not be proof of his divine sonship. On the contrary, attempting to go beyond the laws and boundaries of normal human existence would constitute a wrongful testing of God because it would challenge God to prove that his transcendent power exceeds that of earth's gravity.

Both these temptations are definitively rebutted throughout the Gospels in numerous accounts that picture Jesus being hungry and thirsty and attentive to the needs of those in the same state. These culminate in the mysterious affirmation of his presence in those who hunger and thirst today (Matthew 25:35–45). They do not need divine intervention; they need ours. They put us, not God to the test. So although we, too, should pray that we not be tested, it happens continually through the presence among us of those who are hungry, thirsty, naked, sick, and in prison. When we think about them, we are to remember that Jesus is mysteriously present in them today.

The Third Test

The third test was similarly double-edged.

> Again the devil takes him to a very high mountain and
> shows him all the empires of the world and their splen-
> dor, and says to him, "I'll give you all these if you will
> kneel down and pay homage to me."
>
> Finally Jesus says to him, "Get out of here, Satan!
> Remember, it is written, *You shall pay homage to the Lord
> your God, and him alone shall you serve."*
>
> Then the devil leaves him. . . . (Matthew 4:8–11)

This test makes the clearest distinction between the
koinon of imperial power and the *koinonia* of the Father's
empire. The former entails paying homage to the devil:
in return for which Jesus would receive power over all the
empires of the civilized world and with it, their glory. Jesus
was notionally as free as we are to pay such homage. And
by that gesture he would gain all the military, financial,
and legal powers associated with all the empires that had
enslaved Israel: from the Pharaohs to the Romans. The real
and potential effects of this power on his land, his people,
and his life were plain to see.

Again and again, Jesus refuses to pay homage to such
power. To do so would mean breaking his people's covenant with the God who delivered them from one imperial
power, Egypt, and left them free to love, serve and worship
only that God (Deuteronomy 6:13). This is a God who does
not directly intervene, but leaves us the ethical freedom to
make choices and live with the consequences. After Jesus
refuses the *koinon* of imperial power, the devil leaves him.

In all three tests, Jesus is portrayed as thinking like a
recognizable first-century observant Jew. That means that
the writer of the story uses them to draw lessons from the
history of his people, their current situation, and their

present understanding of their relationship with God. He knows they hope for a Messiah who will not only save them from Roman rule but also re-establish Israel's privileged and powerful place among the nations. But in the light of his understanding of Jesus, he dismisses all such anti-imperial expectations *rooted in violence*. In other words, he rejects for all time those apocalyptic messianic expectations that implicitly, or indeed explicitly, look for a Messiah who will slay Israel's enemies, miraculously end hunger, inspire proper belief, and rule over Israel and all other peoples.[8]

Against such expectation, Jesus is portrayed as rejecting any image of an omnipotent, almighty God. At the same time he accepts the power bestowed on him at his baptism—that of nurturing, nonviolent love. Instead of imperial rule, he prays and lives for a kingdom to come in which God's rule will mean that the hungry are fed, the thirsty given drink, the naked clothed, the sick cared for, and the prisoner and the stranger in the land treated with compassion (Matthew 25:34–45). That is the test on which we shall all be judged.

In his responses to being tested by God, Jesus shows us that a "No" to the devil is also a "Yes" to being human, to the real and personal character of a freely chosen relationship with God. His "No" is also a refusal to claim divine sonship if that means exemption from "the conditions of existence" that include being dependent on earth to sustain us and reliant on our living, reciprocal relationships with each other. In other words, Jesus says "Yes" to being an earthly being and "No" to what we imagine as a heavenly status. For that would exclude him from the community of life on earth.

Such a community does not come into being because people have feelings for each other—though that is required too—but rather when all of them stand in a living, reciprocal relationship to a single living centre and to one another.[9]

10

ENVISIONING JESUS

And Jesus returned in the power of the Spirit
into Galilee. . . . And he came to Nazareth where
he had been brought up and he went to the
synagogue, as his custom was, on the Sabbath day.
And he stood up to read; and there was given to
him the book of the prophet Isaiah. He opened it
and found the place where it was written:
> The Spirit of the Lord is upon me, because he has
> anointed me to preach good news to the poor.
> He has sent me to proclaim release to the captives
> And recovery of sight to the blind,
> To set at liberty those who are oppressed
> To proclaim the acceptable year of the Lord. (Isaiah
> 61:1–2)

And he closed the book and gave it back to the
attendant and sat down; and the eyes of all in
the synagogue were fixed on him. And he began
to say to them: Today this Scripture has been
fulfilled in your hearing.
—Luke 4:14, 16–21

Although scholars have pointed out historic inconsisten-
cies in this narrative,[1] it is evident from the preceding account of Jesus' testing in the desert that what we know as
verifiable history was not the primary concern of the evangelists. Enough is known, however, about the first-century
CE setting for us to discern how those in the Nazareth synagogue would have seen Jesus.

In both Matthew and Luke he goes straight from the desert to Galilee and arrives in his hometown of Nazareth. Those in the synagogue may or may not have heard what others had reportedly witnessed: that he had been baptized by John in the Jordan, where the Spirit of God had descended on him. Nor could they possibly know of the report that the same Spirit had driven him into the wilderness to be tested by the devil—or that he had returned to Nazareth in the power of that Spirit.

They do, of course, know that he is the son of Joseph the carpenter and that he is reported to have worked miracles of healing in Capernaum. But when he read that passage from Isaiah and commented on it, they no doubt mistook him to be claiming to be the Messiah, the Anointed One. In fact he was simply saying that Isaiah's promises were being fulfilled.

Their initial reaction reflects their acceptance of him as a Messianic miracle-worker. So they voice their approval of what he has said while marveling at it. Then another reaction kicks in: Isn't this Joseph's son, one of our own? And if, as reports have it, he is a miracle-worker, surely we can expect him to do miracles for us just as he has done elsewhere?

None of this surprises Jesus, even though he is there not to fulfill their expectations of him as "one of us" but to act as a prophet. But no prophet, he acknowledges, is accepted in his own country. He reminds them that during a severe famine in Israel, the prophet Elijah went only to the house of a widow in Zarephath and, during an outbreak of leprosy in Israel, the prophet Elisha cured only an outsider, Naaman the Syrian.

This provokes the third and final reaction in his audience: rage. It is so great that they hustle him out of the synagogue, out of the town, and toward the brow of a nearby hill, intending to hurl him headlong to his death. But he slips from their grasp and gets away.[2]

It doesn't matter that Luke got the geography wrong—for Nazareth is not built on or near a hill. What matters, and still rings true, is their disappointment and rage at having their hopes dashed. We can understand this, even though we have already been told by both Luke and Matthew that Jesus had refused the powers offered by the devil, and in particular those that reflect the authority, violence, and military glory of this world's empires. Yet this was the image of power attributed to the Messiah and hoped for by many Jews. It was also the direct opposite of the prophetic image from Isaiah envisioned by Jesus.

Nearly two thousand years later, Dietrich Bonhoeffer, a prophetic prisoner for whom there was to be no release from captivity other than death, compared and contrasted these images:

> And the only way to be honest is to recognize that we have to live in the world *etsi deus non daretur* [as if there were no God]. And this is just what we do see—before God! So our coming of age forces us to a true recognition of our situation vis-à-vis God. God is teaching us that we must live as men who can get along very well without him. The God who is with us is the God who forsakes us (Mark 15:34). The God who makes us live in this world without using him as a working hypothesis is the God before whom we are ever standing. Before God and with him we live without God. God allows himself to be edged out of the world and on to the cross. God is weak and powerless in the world and that is exactly the way, the only way in which he can be with us and help us. Matthew 8:17 makes it crystal clear that it is not by his omnipotence that Christ helps us, but by his weakness and suffering.[3]

This modern version of the prophetic criticism of imperial power enforced through violence employs the reverse
strategy exemplified in the paradigm of the suffering servant (Isaiah 40–55). Rather than using God as a working
hypothesis, a hypothetical figure whose power "works"
on our behalf, we begin by expecting nothing from a God
who, in Jesus, is revealed as powerless before the powers of
this world.

This brings us to a question at the heart of our religious
life: is it centered on a Messiah of imperial power, or on
Jesus, the power-rejecting Messiah? We must choose between shocking depictions of bloody massacres inflicted
in the name of God and universalist and peaceful actions
undertaken in the same name—that is, between *koinon* and
koinonia. As Crossan says, the ambiguity of divine power
suffuses the Christian Bible. God's vision of nonviolent justice, offered and embodied in Jesus, is obscured again and
again by the normalcy of civilization's program of religion,
war, and victory—or more succinctly, peace through victory. And that struggle between two transcendental visions
is depicted *within the Bible itself.*[4]

Alas, an historic choice between these visions was made
long ago on behalf of would-be followers of Jesus as Messiah
or Christ. It followed from the takeover of Christianity by
imperial Rome that imposed creeds on mainline Christian
traditions in which a Jesus-free abstraction rules our rituals
and so our expectations of God. The abstraction is con-
tained and celebrated in the oft-repeated formula, "only
begotten Son of the Father, conceived by the Holy Spirit,
born of the Virgin Mary, suffered under Pontius Pilate and
died for us men and for our salvation."

> The creeds emphasize his supernatural origin, then cut
> right from his birth to his death and resurrection. They
> lack all mention of his living and speaking and loving,

of his preaching, healing and prophecy. Not a whis-
per . . . This *lack* became the very stuff of piety.[5]

Catherine Keller's remarks came to mind when I read the
following passage on our relationship to Jesus and his to us:

> It is often asked today whether our spiritual life should
> be "God-centered" or "Christ-centered." Eckhart would
> answer: it should be centered *on* God, *in* Christ. We
> should not see Christ so much as an external figure of
> worship and devotion but as one with whom we are
> *already* united the moment we enter the Ground of the
> Soul. We then share in his relationship with the Father;
> we are sons in the Son. (Note: no daughters in the
> Spirit. Indeed, no Spirit.)
>
> Therefore Eckhart does not encourage us to become
> "Christ-centered" in the sense of being exclusively
> preoccupied with the historical figure, the Aramaic-
> speaking Galilean rabbi who wandered about ancient
> Palestine in a white robe.[6]

This "historical figure" is not even given the courtesy of
his name! Creeds are indeed important historical witnesses
to past and present forms of unifying belief, that is, of a
koinon of doctrinal unity. From Constantine to Eckhart and
on to today, that *koinon* has been preserved largely through
the work and preaching of a clerically educated male elite
who themselves received their doctrine in this creed-based
language. As Keller says, it is all frame, no portrait. It is not
founded on a contemporary vision of a creation-centered
unity that has been cultivated and given form and substance by advances in biblical studies and other branches
of learning.

Relying only on this framework, we have been given
expectations of the Christ figure similar to those of the
Nazarenes in the synagogue; and in much the same way
those expectations lead us to reject Joseph and Mary's son

in favor of being "sons in the Son" (of God). In this divine begetting, there is no maternal nurturing of daughters or by mothers, no room for a Jesus who portrays Samaritans as good neighbors and asks a Samaritan woman for a drink. Instead we are led to expect a Messiah quite different from the one anointed by the Spirit to bring the good news to the poor, pardon to prisoners, sight to the blind, and freedom to the oppressed. As Bonhoeffer knew, in our distress we look for the power of God in the world. But, as he also knew, the Bible directs us to "the powerlessness and suffering of God."[7]

For the truth is that it depends on where in the Bible you look for a Messianic vision and how you interpret what you find. The title of an exhaustive study by Willard M. Swartley speaks for itself: *Slavery, Sabbath, War and Women: Case Issues in Biblical Interpretation*. In each instance Swartley shows how commentators have used the Bible both negatively and positively to support their own predispositions. After a detailed consideration of biblical interpretations that are invoked to support pacifist and non-pacifist arguments against and for waging war, he sums up their ambiguities by pointing out that it is impossible to characterize one position as correct and the others as wrong. Both one's political-economic-social perspective and one's religious tradition play powerful roles in determining how one reads the Bible. Conservative interpretation stresses biblical teaching on authority and patriotism, exalts law over liberation in the Exodus narratives, and applies much of the Bible individually. Liberal interpretation values liberty and equality, sees in the Bible the progress of humanity toward liberal ideals, and uses the Exodus narratives to support freedom guaranteed by democratic institutions. Radical interpretation accents impartial justice, economic freedom to support the needy, and the liberation of the oppressed.[8]

Yet amid the welter of these often conflicting values, one positive symbol has meaning for the whole of humanity: peace. Panikkar is surely correct in declaring peace to be the most universal unifying symbol possible. But within today's military-industrial global complex it is not possible to speak meaningfully about peace without mentioning disarmament—including its nuclear, military, and economic aspects. Also needed is cultural disarmament, that is, a rhetorical and moral reformation of the prevailing culture of domination, whether political, economic, gender-based, religious, or agricultural. Within prevailing cultural parameters, where "armament" signals "defense" and weapons are controlled, used and paid for by "Defense" Ministries, disarmament looks like an improbable folly. Yet surely we should have learned from the past six thousand years, as well as from the aftermath of two World Wars and an oxymoronic "Cold War," that peace cannot be attained through war:

> Peace is not achieved through a treaty, just as love is not reached through a decree. There is something in the nature of peace, just as in that of love, that is withdrawn from commandment. A whole view of reality in general, and of humanity in particular, is at stake. . . . It is a matter of striking a middle course between the belief that humans are good (so that anarchism will be the answer) and that we are bad (and one must defend oneself at all cost). Let us not forget that the *culture of certitude*, inaugurated in the West by Descartes, leads logically to a *civilization of security*—modern society's prevailing ideology. . . . Saint Augustine calls peace the *incertum bonum* [the uncertain good].[9]

Two other issues must be considered here. One is the fact that discussions of war and disarmament generally ignore their effects on the global environment. "Peace *on earth"* is the defining characteristic of an attitude toward the global environment that supports all forms of life within it, including ours. It defines not only our lives here, but, as Ramon Panikkar says, our conception of eternity:

> To put it in very much simplified terms, if you do not believe in an afterlife, what you actualize of life on earth becomes the ultimate and the definitive—becomes a religious matter; if you do believe in another life, its enjoyment in heaven will depend on what you have been on earth. If the earthly is the springboard to the heavenly, then earth also acquires defining characteristics: the earthly peace that has enabled me to live a good life will acquire a religious importance as well.[10]

The second issue is closely connected to this and can be very simply stated. We are one of a multitude of species inhabiting the earth in relationships characterized by interdependence and mutual vulnerability. Our relationships with them define what we have become, what we are, and what we may become. Cultivating unity in peace within the whole of creation is the defining characteristic of *koinonia*. As evidenced in the Great Pergamon Frieze, the defining characteristic of an imperial *koinon* is the victory of military power over this creative unity between us, Earth/ Gaia and her other-than-human beings. It is the antithesis of "good news" to the poor, to all future generations and ultimately, to the whole of creation.

The Identity of Jesus

Freeing the oppressed from the terror, pain and captivity of war is part of the messianic age whose arrival Jesus declared in the synagogue. Theologically, this takes us back to a question posed by Stephen Patterson:

> What sort of God would one believe in if this God were to be seen in Jesus' words and actions?[11]

The answer depends on how we understand the relationship between the human Jesus and a biblical Messiah. Like those in the synagogue, we must learn that he is not eitheror, but both-and. For us too, our notions of what *kind* of biblical Messiah we hope for is decisive: put quite simply, is it one who, as in Bonhoeffer's vision, helps us to cultivate peace in unity not by wielding omnipotent power but by sharing his weakness, suffering, and healing compassion.

That brings us up against the paradox of the Christian doctrine of the Incarnation. It combines two mutually exclusive identities in the person of Jesus: the Galilean son of Joseph and Mary living and preaching in Galilee and the Messiah or Christ, the Anointed One, the only begotten Son of the Father. The Incarnation is a paradox because it presents us simultaneously with qualities or concepts that together create something we can grasp without being quite able to explain or understand it. We may call it the mystery of God. To open it up to scrutiny, as I have done here, is not to destroy it, but to expose the historically constructed presuppositions we bring to it.

Consider the analogy of light and darkness: if we keep them in focus together, the light shows up the darkness for what it is—the absence of light. Similarly, the light is intensified in the presence of darkness. But each retains its own presence and importance. If we merge them, we don't get any more clarity of vision, only grey. If we concentrate on one and ignore the other, we lose our vision of the whole. If we lose sight either of Jesus or of Christ, we lose the mystery of the Incarnation, a mystery we believe to be created and generated by God and nurtured in the Spirit.

Just as a change in the weather involves both the preceding and the succeeding weather conditions, so during a time of necessary change in theology the identification of Jesus with the Christ cannot be brushed aside and does not lose its importance. The frame does not dissolve but cracks open within it. For some of us, what comes into view may not be the historical Jesus but his Messianic concern for the poor in all their various needs. And at a time when conflicts, wars, and social militarization support a global arms industry devastating to earth's life-giving resources, each of us needs to hear Jesus' unqualified command to forgive our enemies and respond by invoking his blessing on the peacemakers.

For those of us struggling to hold Jesus and the Christ together, the symbolic role of the Spirit of *koinonia* takes on a new importance. She not only hovers over Jesus/Christ, but watches over each of us, promoting peace between us by revealing that "the gentiles are also heirs, members of the same body and sharers of the promise in Christ Jesus through the gospel" (Ephesians 3:5–6). She gives us more than logic or certitude, more than knowledge of texts and their interpretations can give. She gives us a sense of what Bonhoeffer described as participating in the being of Jesus because—and this is an important contemporary insight—he participated in our being, in our being human. And therefore we can now participate in his relationships with God through the Spirit. This, for me, is "the Ground of the Soul"—the soil, bread, water, air, energy, and spirit we share with each other just as Jesus shared them with those around him.

The outcome of such a shared engagement—of sinking ourselves at length and in quietness in the birth, life, sayings, and death of Jesus—is a strategic reversal of the usual Christian expectations of the power and wisdom of God. The revelation of God in the brutal ordinariness of a life lived under Roman imperial rule and a death imposed by its military arm ensures that it is a revelation *of God*, not the fulfillment of our desires or ambitions. So it was for Bonhoeffer under the brutal ordinariness of life in a Nazi prison and a death imposed by the SS.

This is a key to deciphering the meaning of what the Jesus of the Gospels calls "the Father's empire." As an ordinary Jew he shared an historic orientation towards Yahweh's steadfast love. He proclaimed a God who gave freedom to prisoners, sight to the blind, and joy to the sorrowful. He preached a God who blesses the poor and the peacemakers, remembers each sparrow, feeds the ravens, clothes the flowers, and takes note of a bruised reed, valuing each one of them and each one of us.

But given Jesus' context, that of the Roman Empire and its brutally destructive and overwhelming power, it becomes clear that he uses the word "empire" paradoxically. On his lips, the word reverses all routine expectations of divine power and of God's empire. It confers royalty on outcasts—the very ones who are the victims of the world's political and economic power. It states that God chose outsiders like Naaman the Syrian, symbol of those deprived of power through religious authority, wealth, education, high birth, and culture, over those who have all these advantages.[12] And it means that in God's empire all other-than-human members of the community of life on earth are valued for their intrinsic worth, for what they are in themselves.

Such immersion in the sayings attributed to Jesus leads us from the paradoxical insights of language *about* Jesus onto study of the language *of* Jesus, in particular his use of parable. For paradox is the formal principle of parable. This is why biblical scholars stress the foundational role of primary texts in any contemporary re-envisioning of Jesus. His parables, aphorisms, and dialogues give us insights into his vision of God and God's empire. Such a vision comes, says Robert Funk, in bits and pieces, in random stunning insights rather than in continuous articulated wholes. Yet they are more than the sum of their parts. For from such fragments of insight we can begin to piece together some sense of the shape of the whole, some idea of the nature of "the once and future Jesus."[13]

For example, we can ask what kind of flesh-and-blood person would enjoin us as he did when he said,

Love your enemies;

Turn the other cheek;

The Father's empire belongs to the poor.[14]

Could these texts be attributed to a bearer of imperial power? To Herod, Constantine or their political, military and ecclesiastical successors? To hear Jesus speak about an already-present Kingdom gives some idea, some evidence of the kind of God we can expect to be present in the here and now. The historic, biblical past of this kingdom runs from the Messianic hopes and expectations of the prophets—in a time when swords will be turned into ploughshares—to the appearance of Jesus. With him it comes alive as an event upon the present world stage rather than a spiritualized beyond. In this expansion of hope to include the whole world, the intentions and expectations of the prophets, of Jesus, of Bonhoeffer, of Aung San Suu Kyi, and of all who cultivate unity through peace, achieve their proper development.[15] This takes on a particular urgency in a time of global climatic crisis.

11

SACRED UNITY

The more we ask, search, and test our answers, the deeper the questions take us. Yet as the questions deepen, the answers that we gather do not simply crumble; only the false certainties do that.
—Catherine Keller, *God and Power*, p. 150

But why should transcendence be thought of as an opposite to immanence? I suggest that, rather than being an argument for the separation of the divine and the material, it is instead a consequence of that supposed separation.
—Grace Jantzen, *Becoming Divine*, p. 270

What was it like in first century Galilee to hear the story of Jonah or to hear Jesus use images of the kingdom of God that raised questions about Jewish expectations of kingship after David? His metaphorical imagery presents God not as a Lord and King to be served in fear but as a compassionate Father:

> Be full of pity, just as your Father . . . is full of pity. (Q/ Luke 6:36; Matthew 5:48)

His central exhortation to love one's enemies (rather than kill them) is based on what he sees as God's conduct:

> Love your enemies and pray for those persecuting you so that you may become sons of your Father; for he raises his sun on bad and good, and rains on the just and unjust.' (Q 6:27; Matthew 5:44–45; Luke 6:27–28, 35c–d)

There is a striking correlation between Jesus' own conduct, what he advocates in his sayings, and the way that he conceives God. He exemplifies what it meant for a Jew of his generation to *hear* the prophetic call of Isaiah or the parable of Jonah: it meant listening to the words *and* taking their intention to heart. In particular, he grasps what it means to see God as non-discriminatory—that is, as concerned for the welfare of those we deem bad or unjust as for those we deem good or just. Furthermore, we are to be concerned not only about those we consider—or who consider themselves—chosen by God, but about those presumed to be pagans and outcasts. And last but not least, we must be concerned for the welfare of all species of living beings—human and non-human alike.

It is not surprising, says James Robinson, that Jesus' shocking view of God has largely been ignored, as has his corresponding ethic. For this understanding of God transcends the common-sense justice of reward and punishment that pervaded antiquity and still pervades human cultures today. And as we saw in the parable of Jonah, it also transcends the prevailing prophetic expectation of God's actions in regard to the oppressors of Israel and Judah—nations whose people considered themselves God's favorites. It now transcends any theological argument within Christian communities for the concept of retaliation as a basis for—or even an intrinsic part of—the ethical order.

To prescribe the love of enemies on the grounds of God's impartiality toward foe as well as friend was indeed very unusual. And, says Robinson, it is striking that on this most central point Jesus did not derive his unusual vision of God and his highest ethic from the major Hebrew scriptures or indeed from anywhere in the cultural landscape of the Ancient Near East. The Matthean antithesis makes this clear:

> You have heard that it was said, "You shall love your
> neighbor and hate your enemy." But I say to you, "Love
> your enemies. . . ." (Matthew 5:43–44a)

Love of enemies does indeed fly in the face of the common-sense judgment that the punishment should fit the
crime. Against that, as Robinson points out, Jesus' rare view
of God and its resultant radical ethic is rooted not in human judgment but in his experience of the world around
him where the climate on the wrong side of the tracks
behaves in the same way as the climate on the right side.
What was unusual was that Jesus drew such a radical ethic
from this simple observation of everyday weather patterns.
There God is clearly "in charge," and shows us how she
and therefore we should act: with kindness to all, the bad
as well as the good.[1]

Today, when we have so much information about how
climate actually works, our own contributions to it and its
effects on others, this challenge to our ethics looms larger
than ever. We, too, are beginning to understand that *koinonia* calls for the positive cultivation of a unity *that is already
there*. The birds know it, the fish in the sea know it. The sun
and the rain know it. If we now say that we, too, know it,
how, if at all, does our knowledge of this unification affect
our ethics? How does it affect our vision of God?

As became clear in the Cornelius episode, some of Jesus'
followers remained true to the vision of a God who makes
no distinctions between us or between us and all living
beings. It is a vision that at least potentially unites us religiously, ethically, and physically, and undergirds the same
cultivation of unity that identified the early followers of
Jesus *as* his followers.

Living out of this vision highlights not only the effec-
tiveness of Jesus' use of parable, but also his embodiment of
it. He lived it as well as spoke it, challenging accepted conventions and expectations that God's power and presence

were "otherworldly," that is, attached to a heavenly rather than an earthly realm. He used "this-worldly" symbolic discourse to connect the Father's empire to the actual world in which we live and to all the conditions of our existence. This leverage on the real is the intrinsic link between his parables, his images of God, and the actuality of his life and our lives. It argues against, indeed forbids, detaching the person and words of Jesus from his natural, earthly context. It argues for an ever-deepening understanding of a Judeo-Christian ethic based on the command: *"Hear, O Israel: the Lord our God is one God"* (Deuteronomy 6:4).

Therefore the figure of the parabler himself becomes the focus of our attention. What happens "at the centre in the words" focuses our attention on the one who speaks them. Here too, as Funk says, what one sees is determined in no small degree by the way one looks, by the connection between the phenomenon to be observed and how one brings it into view.[2] In short, by bringing Jesus into view as parabler, one comes to see him also as parable, as a parable of the God whose immanent/transcendent kingdom stands opposed to the *koinon* of imperial power experienced by Ninevite, Greek, Roman, and Jew alike.

This view of Jesus is not new. It was expressed very clearly after his death when Paul proclaimed the Cross of Jesus as the supreme Parable and the risen Jesus as the Parable of God:

> For Jews demand signs and Greeks seek wisdom, but we preach Christ crucified, a stumbling block to Jews and folly to Gentiles, but to those who are called, both Jew and Greek, Christ the power of God and the wisdom of God. (1 Corinthians 1:22–24)

The Pauline antitheses of "stumbling block/power" and "folly/wisdom" resound with the imaginative shock, the shattering of expectation associated with parable. As does the simultaneous identification of a routinely crucified man with the power and wisdom of God. Crossan comments:

> There was the Cross, and the immediate conclusion was that it represented the divine rejection of Jesus. But if Jesus' parabolic vision was correct, then the Cross itself was not rejection but was itself the great Parable of God. . . . The Cross replaced the parables and became in their place the supreme Parable. . . . All this Paul explained to the Corinthians. . . . Jesus died as parabler and rose as Parable.[3]

Kierkegaard, however, stresses both the death of Jesus *and* its essential continuity with his earthly identity, character, and life. He sees this as the fundamental theological paradox of Christianity:

> That God has existed in human form, has been born, grown up, and so forth, is surely the paradox *sensu strictissima*, the absolute paradox. . . . [I]n connection with the absolute paradox the only understanding possible is that it cannot be understood. . . . [S]peculative philosophy cannot get hold of it at all. . . . [I]t merely thrusts the understanding away in the interests of inwardness in existing.[4]

Kierkegaard sees that the absolute paradox of God existing in human form stops philosophical speculation in its tracks. And if paradox is the formal principle of parable, the life of Jesus is a parable of God. The only way to understand it is to recognize that it cannot be understood either as a philosophical argument about transcendence/immanence or a scientific proposition on the nature of matter. To use a contemporary phrase, it does not compute. It does, however, offer insights into the sacred unity of God with "all things" and its particular but not singular embodiment in Jesus. This means that his parables cannot be analyzed as a set of propositions but are an "event" in and through which one's very existence is transformed.

⊙⊙

For Kierkegaard the absolute paradox posed by the God-man was the Archimedean point on which his existence turned.[5] As we saw, the same was true for Bonhoeffer. The paradox of Jesus as truly God and truly human remains discernible in the writings of the early Church Fathers, but they couched it in abstract philosophical terms rather than in narrative or poetic language. From the fourth century Nicene Creed to the fifth century Chalcedonian Creed, paradox was used to describe Jesus formally: as one who, from the moment of his conception, is *at the same time* complete in Godhead and in manhood:

> Our Lord Jesus Christ, *at once* complete in Godhead and complete in manhood, truly God and truly man, . . . be-gotten of Mary the Virgin, recognized *in two natures, without confusion, without change, without division, without separation.* [6] (italics added)

What could be more paradoxical or parabolic than saying that Jesus *simultaneously* embodies the normatively incompatible concepts of divinity and humanity: from the first moments of his existence in Mary's womb to the moment of his death on the cross? The *is/is not* of metaphor, the *either/or* of human and divine is held together without, as common sense would require, separating or dividing them one from the other. To let either one go would be to surrender to literalism and lose the continuity of identity between Jesus' earthly existence and God.

So far, so good. For those unaccustomed to such terminology, however, the abstractness of this philosophically sophisticated theological response to the mystery of Jesus' life is a barrier rather than an opening to any shared experience of the mystery it seeks to express. It does not get into the hearer's consciousness, nor does it offer time for her to feel its imaginative shock. It lacks poetic imagery that would draw us on to further unexpressed and ultimately inexpressible insight. The many-layered meaning of its unadorned, almost matter-of-fact conceptual language was and remains familiar and accessible to no more than a very limited audience among Christians. In that respect, nothing has changed since the fifth century CE.

Therefore creedal statements based on this language were and are conversation stoppers—rather than starters—for most Christians, and certainly for non-Christians. For they bring together baldly and succinctly two opposing views of reality: what we can presume to know about the nature of human beings, and what we think we know about the nature of God. We normally deal with this clash of views by choosing one rather than the other. In other words, we make what appears to be a reasonable choice between them based on our knowledge of or arguments for one rather than the other. Culturally too, certain factors come into play. At Christmas, there is a welcome but all too brief emphasis on Jesus' birth and family ties. This cannot, however, compensate for the erasure of the female and of the human body in the fourth-century doctrine of a transcendent God who is Father, Son and Spirit. This became the basis for a theology that emphasizes the mystery of a God accessible only through belief and fundamentally defined by bodily absence.[7]

For the most part, therefore, Christian ritual and discourse have caused the human person and personality of Jesus to recede into the background as he is routinely addressed simply as "Christ, the Son of God."

So by degrees, Kierkegaard noted,

> All pith and vigour was distilled out of Christianity; the tension of the paradox was relaxed and one became a Christian without noticing it and without any possibility of offence. It became as simple as thrusting a foot in a stocking. What we specially praise in Christ is precisely what one would be most embittered by if we were his contemporaries. We are content to admire and

praise, and maybe (as was said of a scrupulous translator who rendered an author word for word and therefore lost the meaning) "too conscientious," also too cowardly and feeble of heart really to wish to understand. Christendom has done away with Christianity without being quite aware of it.[8]

In Kierkegaard's distinction between Christianity and Christendom we find a clue to what happened not only to our image of Jesus, but also to his image of the kingdom of God. Christendom was inaugurated by the conversion of Constantine to Christianity, for the Roman Empire then became "Christian-dom" and the divine domain became indistinguishable from the imperial one. With that distinction lost, the kingdom of God came to be identified with the image of a royal, divinely constituted domain embodying a *koinon* of imperial splendor and military power that defeats and enslaves rather than forgives enemies. As such, it represents everything inimical to Jesus' own vision of the kingdom of God.

Instead, Christendom became a religious hierarchical domain in which creedal statements about "our Lord Jesus Christ" were (and are) taken as evidence of faith in him rather than as paradoxical expressions of his presence among us and the demands it lays upon us. If, as Kierkegaard saw, neither rational thought nor speculative philosophy can get hold of what the creeds proclaim, neither can our imaginative faculties. The only understanding available to us is that their supposed certainties cannot be argued against. Unlike an ordinary riddle, the conundrum has no possible answer. The "pith and vigor" of the mystery is lost, and we become too feeble (or bored?) even to wish to understand it.

Ricoeur is rather more hopeful; he aims to keep the mystery alive by calling on our imagination:

> Where the understanding fails, imagination still has the power to present our ideas in images that "give us more to think about."[9]

Productive imagination enables an ongoing interior conversation that explores and grasps, *without being able to define*, the truth concealed in the paradox of the Incarnation. This offers a positive response to the ultimate mystery that confronts us in the life story of Jesus: we learn to hear it, experience it, and accept it for what it is: a parable of God. It becomes a story event that gets into the hearer's consciousness and is felt in its full force only when it is too late to do much about it. One can tell oneself stories but not parables, just as one cannot fool oneself with a riddle one has just invented.[10]

Historically, however, what was heard, learnt, and affirmed were paradoxical creedal statements offered by ecclesiastical academic elites as ways of defining the *divinity* of Jesus. Their inevitable failure to produce rationally acceptable conclusions about that divinity, on the basis of paradoxical formulas such as those of Chalcedon, affected those far beyond their closed circle. In time, as we know, this debacle led to schism between Churches, and eventually to violence and religiously sanctioned hatred of other Christians who uphold different formulas—a violence that persists even to the present day.

This has had two particular effects. Firstly, it has directed attention away from Jesus' own person onto normatively incompatible creedal concepts of divinity and humanity, for one can accurately define divinity only as the opposite of humanity and vice versa. Secondly, it has focused attention onto the formulaic language that was and continues to be used to talk about the Christ rather than attending to Jesus' own words and their parabolic character. The emphasis on statements about him has concentrated attention on the human logic of law and punishment, equality and equivalence. It has thereby obscured or even replaced the logic of excess and of divine generosity used by Jesus.[11]

In short, the move from the language *of* Jesus to language *about* Christ began with Paul, continued on into the Church Councils before and after Chalcedon, and has dominated Christian ecclesiastical and theological language up to the present day. This linguistic constraint has affected and continues to affect the terms in which the paradox of Jesus, "complete in manhood and in Godhead," was and is described. The problem with those terms is that they are used, debated, and "understood"—as if that were possible—only by a sophisticated, highly educated elite. Indeed, by no means all of those present at the Council of Chalcedon understood what the Greek terms used in their Creed could possibly mean. And it's "all Greek" to us, too.

The linguistic barrier rises higher still in the complexities of language used to describe the Trinitarian relationships imagined to unite Father, Son, and Spirit and to connect them and "the world." The use of terms like "immanence" and "transcendence" as basic concepts—although often in directly opposing senses—has left the great majority of Christians not only untouched but quite predictably uncomprehending. Karl Rahner, for instance, uses "immanence" where Jürgen Moltmann uses "transcendence" and "economic" where Moltmann uses "immanence." This terminological impasse in regard to the relationships between the "Persons" of the Trinity has also affected perceptions of our own relationship to Jesus. Above all, it has left us ignorant of or uninterested in the parabolic narratives through which he communicated his own paradoxical understanding of the mystery of our relationships with the Spirit within the Father's empire.

The Event of Parable

Today, however, we benefit from an increased library of ancient written material, such as the Gospel of Thomas, and from extensive research into what happens in a parable "event." Gaston Bachelard, for example, uses the linguistic, aesthetic distinction between mind and soul to alert us to the nature of such events. He points out that in many languages, mind and soul (*der Geist und die Seele*) are not synonymous. In this context the word *Geist* refers to the mind. *Seele*, which means "soul," is a word born of our breath. (Try it!) Its vocal importance arrests our attention and initiates a physical, earthy commitment to grasping some understanding of an entire poem or parable. And that is where the mind takes over.

This commitment is more relaxed, less cerebral than a consciousness associated solely with the mind and expressed in formulaic mode. The force manifest in poems and in parables does not pass immediately through the circuits of knowledge. Its metaphoric resonances are dispersed on different planes of our life and the repercussions invite us to give greater depth to our own existence.

> In the resonance we hear the poem, in the reverberations as we speak it, it is our own: The reverberations bring about a change of being. It is as though the poet's being were our being.[12]

This is another way of describing the "conversation" between speaker and hearer initiated by parable. Parable is akin to poetry in that images created by the parabler enable the audience to "live out" something that they may or may not have experienced and to feel its resonances at different levels of their own being. The poet John Keats used the concept of "negative capability" to describe what occurs. We become capable, he said, of contemplating the world in its uncertainties, mysteries, and doubts without reaching after fact or reason to reconcile its contradictory aspects; or to fit it into closed or rational systems (Keats 1817).

> The Temple bell stops,
> But the sound
> Keeps coming—
> Out of the flowers (Basho)

How many of Jesus' hearers had travelled the road from Jerusalem to Jericho and been set upon by thieves? Yet the image of this traveler and his Samaritan rescuer reverberated with those who heard Jesus speak, and can reverberate with those who hear his words today. We do not need to rationalize, experience, or even describe the feelings aroused in us by the story, for like all poetic images it eludes objective critical attitudes or analyses. It touches the depths before it stirs the surface.[13]

In Jesus' lifetime the resonances and reverberations among those who heard him were so deep that his parables were remembered and, as they were rehearsed to others, more or less faithfully re-heard and rehearsed. And so with slightly different nuances, they were passed on to future generations. The "fresh bread" of parables lately discovered in *The Gospel of Thomas*, for instance, has refreshed and added to our understanding of many familiar ones. Together, these parables have become and remain events shaped by the contexts of different times, places, and religious communities.

While the parable about the Samaritan traveler refers to a particular act of mercy, it makes its impact by offering an ongoing critique of, and indeed an assault upon, conventional hierarchical religious structures and divisions. A similar challenge is presented by the parabolic encounter between Jesus and the Samaritan woman—a text written toward the end of the first century CE and probably unknown to Paul. The continuing impact of these two "events" flows from words and actions through which, given the Jewish hatred of Samaritans at that time, Jesus disrupted conventional notions of who is worthy or unworthy, who is saved or lost, whom we may expect help from and whom we should help.

However, the distance between his world and ours can often mean that we lack a common frame of reference within which we can immediately understand the il/logic of what he said or did. "Worthiness" and "salvation" can and do mean very different things in today's contexts. Therefore we have to translate Jesus' words and actions into contemporary language forms and both literally and metaphorically excavate their settings. Nor can we presuppose a shared religious background or ritual understanding among people today.

Indeed, the opposite is the case. The lack of a shared hinterland becomes an acute problem in a world where instant verbal communication presumes but cannot guarantee instant understanding. (Remember Kierkegaard's translator!) Opportunities to "re-hear" vanish as the speed of communicating through mixed media is accompanied by an unprecedented speed of travel and the potential for social interaction on a global scale. Also at risk is our ability to listen and respond to others—a demanding social skill. It calls for the reading of facial expressions, body language, and speech to interpret what has been said and understand the implied relationships—an immensely complex process. Listening is a great and much underrated skill—except in psychotherapy where it is studied as a discipline and learned as a technique. It requires that personal preoccupations be set aside, if only momentarily, in order to be truly attentive to another person. All of this has become very difficult in today's digital, visual, instant culture, one very

different from the largely oral culture of the small-scale, lo-
cally bounded, and religiously enclosed communities who
saw and *heard* Jesus and his followers speak.

This cultural difference underlies the task involved in
hearing Jesus speak today. The relation between contemporary language and thought and those attributed to Jesus
does not mean belatedly catching up with the thought by
means of the word expressing it. Rather, his words must
once again take on the character of a poetic event. We
have to reverberate with the words until we feel ourselves
re-verbalizing them out of and into our own experience;
we cannot begin by simply aiming for a conceptual grasp
of their meaning. This means that if their imaginative potential is to survive, Jesus' words must be spoken and read
in ways that resonate within the completely different kind
of human logic prevalent in our environment. I find this
potential in the translations that I have used here in retell-
ing the stories of Jonah, Peter and Cornelius.

☙

The real meeting point between Jesus' logic and ours,
between the use of language then and now, is that we
share the same identity as human beings. We have the
same imaginative faculties and depend on the same earth,
sun, and rain to sustain our lives, albeit in seemingly very
different circumstances. We too can discern and use the
difference between metaphors and arguments, and find
contemporary meaning in old metaphors. True, we seldom
see seed sown in fields by hand or a woman kneading (or
needing) to bake bread daily for her household. But the
scientific facts revealed by electron microscopes about the
reproductive qualities of a fungus like yeast can make us
marvel all the more as it "raises" a mound of flour.

The historic nature of biblical language requires that
we translate the truth it reveals into our own language.

This includes the task of redefining, refining, and finding our own language for relating to that truth. The difficulty is that New Testament language has too often come to be heard with the presumption that Jesus spoke and is to be heard not as the son of Joseph, but as the Son of God. Even appearing to claim this identity caused a riot in his home synagogue at Nazareth. Where's the shock now?

If Christian theology is understood as dependent on language *from* God, that is, upon language events as divine revelation attributable to Jesus, then to what extent is talk *about* or *to* God still possible for us today—or permissible? In our multi-religious world, we cannot take for granted that a parabolic event is constitutive of all knowledge of God: or that it is not a word *about* God but *is* Jesus, Word of God.[14] When Jesus is appropriately translated, he becomes the question of whether or not we are willing to be identified with him by cultivating a *koinonia* that presupposes a sacred unity between us and all creatures. Otherwise, as the gospel writers have Jesus say:

> Ninevites will judge this generation and condemn it. For as Jonah was a sign to them of the need for repentance, and they repented, so am I to this generation. Look, something more than Jonah is here! (Matthew 12:41 // Luke 11:32)

12

THE GOD OF JESUS

> What, do you wish to know your Lord's
> meaning in this thing? Know it well, love was
> his meaning. Who reveals it to you? Love. What
> did he reveal to you? Love. Why does he reveal
> it to you? For love. Remain in this, and you
> will know more of the same. But you will never
> know different, without end.
> —Julian of Norwich, *Showings*, p. 342

The implied question put to us by Julian of Norwich was about the role of God in "all his works," including the creation of all things and the death of Jesus. Her comprehensive answer includes "all things that have come to be," including death. In one sense, it is not a satisfactory answer since our experience belies it. But the more we reflect on it, the more comprehensive it appears. It does not allow us to define love satisfactorily, but then neither may we define God in ways more satisfactory to human reason:

> Beloved, let us love one another; for love is of God, and whoever loves is born of God and knows God. Whoever does not love does not know God; for God is love. (1 John 4:7–8)

Julian's answer accepts this understanding of God despite its difficulties. Paul, however, in the first recorded reaction we have to Jesus' death, focuses on whether or not that death makes sense to us, and if not, whether it makes sense to God. He poses the question paradoxically, juxtaposing the concept of "wisdom" with its opposite, "folly." Then he "makes sense" of that by contrasting God's wisdom with ours:

> For since, in the wisdom of God, the world did not know God through wisdom, it pleased God through the folly of what we preach to save those who believe. For Jews demand signs and Greeks seek wisdom, but we preach Christ crucified, a stumbling block [scandal] to Jews and folly to Gentiles, but to those who are called, both Jews and Greeks, Christ the power of God and the wisdom of God. (1 Corinthians 1:21–24)

As a Jewish Roman citizen, Paul knew that those who suffered crucifixion were symbols both of the folly of resistance to Roman power and of its supremacy. To us, Spartacus and his followers may be symbols of heroism, but at the time of their revolt against Rome, the grim reality of their crucifixion was a sign of their defeat by imperial force of arms. Therefore to envision Jesus crucified as "the power and wisdom of God" was, in the eyes of both Jew and Greek, the act of a fool. So to see Jesus as Paul did, rather than simply agreeing with him by default, we must remember that what he says about Jesus he is also saying about God: that the *crucified* Jesus *is* the power and wisdom of God. In effect, he identifies Jesus' God as equally the victim of imperial power.

Identifying God in this way changed Paul's life. It also changed the way he spoke about Jesus' death. Up until then it was a scandal to Jews and foolishness to gentiles. For both, it went against all preconceptions of divine power and wisdom. And if we think about it, it also goes against ours. It turns normal ideas about power upside down because it subverts all rational understanding of either power or wisdom. It is, in the deepest sense, *para-doxa:* that is, against all accepted opinions or beliefs.

Taking this paradoxical view of Jesus' death disorients us, for by contradicting the accepted order of things it undermines our expectations of him and challenges us to readjust them. At the same time it gives us an intuitive insight into the nature of God, one that is inaccessible to rational thought. Responding honestly, we may well exclaim with Ernst Bloch, "I am an atheist—for God's sake!" For the paradoxical image of a powerless God immediately destroys preconceptions about divine power and our ability to trust in it.

Today, the conceptual problem most of us face stems from the fortunate fact that we do not have to endure the brunt of imperial military power. For us, the paradox is expressed in "tired" language, language that requires too much thought and is heavy-laden with presuppositions. Words like *atonement, salvation*, and *redemption* have reduced the paradox of Jesus' death to what it means *for us* rather than what it would mean for our understanding of God in the context of the *koinon* of Rome. Instead of trying to understand more of what Paul is saying, we are forced to try to understand what subsequent translators and interpreters of his words have said. Hart quotes Iris Murdoch: "We are like people who for a long time looked out of a window without noticing the glass—and then one day began to notice this too."[1]

Staying with Paul's reactions forces us to notice the rather smudged glass of commentary and creedal formulations. But how can we go behind it to experience as profoundly as he did that reversal of expectation he expressed so vividly? If there is a more hazardous enterprise than burying a theological word, says Hart, it is surely the attempt to revive one. Yet throughout its history, Christian theology has found it necessary to go back in order to go forward.[2] Julian of Norwich took an important step forward with her attempt to understand and to accept what such a reversal of expectation might mean for our understanding of God.

In his time, Paul was doing the same. We know from his own accounts that his change from being a Jew to being a follower of Jesus was linked directly to a disorienting perception of Jesus crucified. He defined this disorientation in paradoxical terms: as exchanging known and accepted images of imperial-divine power for unacceptable, indeed scandalous images of human-divine weakness. This amounted to exchanging traditional political-religious wisdom for a singular personal insight that would be construed as folly.

But this did not remain simply an individual disorientation. By expressing it as powerfully as he did, Paul effectively reoriented the religious worldview of those nascent Christian communities to whom he preached and with whom he lived and corresponded. We saw this also happen to Cornelius and his household. Peter (however reluctantly) called them to a reorientation of their lives: from a theology of power defined in worldly imperial terms toward one defined by its opposite, from a *koinon* of war to a *koinonia* of peace:

> God issued the message of peace to the Israelites through Jesus Christ (he is the sovereign of all people): . . . Jesus of Nazareth, when God had invested him with the power of the Holy Spirit, went about doing good and healing all who were oppressed by the devil, because God was with him. We can attest to all that Jesus did in Jewish territory and in Jerusalem. There they actually put him to death by hanging him on a tree. (Acts 10:36–38)

Peter's understanding of Jesus' life and death as a "message of peace" is very different from that of Paul. Its content and intent is that of a creed: an attestation of belief in what God had done in Jesus, both in his life and in his death. It is also the first reported instance of the "cultural adaptation" of that message.[3] Now, however, we are so culturally adapted to it that we fail to grasp how shocking it was for Cornelius as an official of the Roman Empire to be told that a crucified Israelite is "Lord of all" (RSV), or "sovereign of all people" (Pervo).

It was even more shocking to be told that this Lord of all brings not a sword, but peace, for such a claim reverses not only political expectations but also religious ones. And if the *given* of revelation is that God reigns supreme, that too was turned upside down by what was revealed in the crucifixion of Jesus. It set total vulnerability *against* accepted use of power over the vulnerable; folly *against* what is regarded as wisdom; healing and doing good *against* military oppression and terror. Then, in God's name, Peter claims that this commitment to vulnerability and the folly of doing good to those in need rather than dealing ruthlessly with them constitutes the preferred route to peace. This is how *koinonia* reverses the effects of *koinon*: through a "sovereign" Jesus who brings peace, not war.

To accept these premises and conclusions meant the uprooting and overthrow of all that had been handed on to Paul, as well as to Peter and Cornelius. Paul's Israelite tradition accorded God the overriding power and wisdom revealed in such events as the Exodus. As we saw with Jonah, even prophets couldn't handle having these presuppositions about the power exercised by their God on their behalf being reversed—especially in such matters as who could be perceived as an enemy and who as a friend—when one was acting in the name of that God.

But the validity of these traditional religious categories as a basis for relationships vanished with Jesus' injunction that enemies were to be loved—that is, no longer related to *as* enemies. Paul also received this unifying message of peace based on love, and he passed it on to the

Corinthians. He had come to understand that giving his body to be burned (or in another version, giving all his goods to the poor) would mean nothing if he did not love. He spelt out the positive qualities brought by love to his relationships with others; patience and kindness instead of arrogance and rudeness; giving way to others rather than insisting on having his own way; not rejoicing in doing wrong but in what is right; bearing all things, hoping all things, enduring all things (1 Corinthians 13:3–13).

There could be no greater contrast between this and his previous understanding of God that had fueled his violent campaign of hate against the followers of Jesus,

> ravaging the church, and entering house after house to drag off men and women and commit them to prison . . . breathing threats and murder against the disciples of the Lord. (Acts 8:3, 9:1)

The younger Paul (Saul) seems to have performed these violent acts under the warrant of the Sanhedrin, and had felt fully justified in persecuting and executing the believers and followers of Jesus (Acts 26:10). We see the physical force he used erupting in the language: *wreaking havoc*, attempting to *obliterate* believers, *dragging* women as well as men to prison! All this attests to his former extreme ferocity.[4] And it was all done, he said, because he was convinced that he ought to do it to "oppose" the name of Jesus of Nazareth! (Acts 26:9)

This gives some idea of the *volte-face* his conversion required of him: it meant denying that violent, legitimating vision of a God of almighty power and accepting the image presented to him in Jesus on the Cross. In other words, he came to see the Cross not only as an instrument for our salvation, with all the difficulties that entails, but—as Julian of Norwich later saw it—as a revelation of love. Paul attributed invisible might and wisdom to a God "throned on high" and had to set these against the visible reality of God "nailed to a cross." His traditional religious orientation toward an invisible God of power was *dis*oriented by the *visible* scandal of the powerlessness of Jesus. Before his eyes (so to speak), God was clearly seen as humanly weak, bereft of strength, subject to imperial power rather than wielding any recognizable form of it.

This disorienting event radically altered Paul's perception of God by dismantling his traditional understanding of divine power. Were we to fully grasp its significance, it could potentially be as upsetting an exercise for us today as it was for Paul. Ray Hart understood this to mean turning over the muck-heap of theology and finding what we can cultivate in it from what has largely been buried there over the centuries:

> Tradition must be dismantled to see what it mediates, what it handed around and hands on. Mediating only in dissolution, tradition furnishes debris for building up the structure to house what it could not hold against the flood of time.[5]

The problem today is the huge accumulation of traditional debris that has been handed on to us. Unlike Paul, our distance from the historical setting of Jesus' death means that later interpretations—those presenting that "scandal" as our salvation rather than as a revelation of a God of peace and love—make it difficult for us to be "disoriented" by the "weakness" of God on the Cross. Also, ever since Constantine co-opted Christianity, the dominant orientation of the western Church has been toward preaching the death-defying power of the risen Lord and attributing it both implicitly and explicitly to divine omnipotence.

This unassailable power is invoked and understood as being exercised by God exclusively and ruthlessly on our behalf. Such a shocking presupposition lies behind the assumption that the same divine "ruthlessness" *toward* Jesus was evident in his being crucified *"for us men* [sic] *and for our salvation."* Furthermore, this theological barter was executed, in every sense, through God's "normal" exercise of imperial power. This implicit presupposition, all the more powerful for being generally unexpressed, has become theologically normative for a Christian vision of God. Fundamental decisions about what can and should be said about God appear to have been already taken, so that in Ray Hart's phrase we are "in bondage to a fated imagination"[6] Paul's "shock" and his consequent conversion to a life lived in love and peace is no longer seen as a fitting response to the parabolic life, words, and death of Jesus. Instead, a sort of complacency about the manner of our salvation has dulled what should be our clear recognition that the routinely held Christian view of God is quite at odds with that of Jesus.

☙

In the first centuries of Christianity, the influence of Peter and Paul, together with the persecution of Christians by the Roman Empire, kept open the question of the nature of God's power revealed in Jesus. But from Nicaea onwards, imperial influences over Church and State ensured that divine power was again symbolized in terms of militarist force against perceived enemies—that is, those perceived as inimical to doctrinal unity. This post-apostolic understanding is shockingly evident in the "Wars of the Cross"—the Crusades. The name speaks for itself. Ruthless Christian Crusaders attacked those seen to attack the *koinon* of Christianity. Similarly, the reign of the Inquisition deployed pitiless Christian interrogators to inflict torture and death on any Christian appearing to question it.

These violent offensives in defense of doctrinal supremacy reflected and reinforced an imperialist perception of

God's power on earth. As such, it was built into church architecture in the form of Crusader tombs and war memorials and proclaimed, celebrated, and hymned in the dogma and liturgy of "Christian soldiers marching as to war"— behind the cross of Jesus. They are kept alive in ecclesiastical protocols and rituals where God is hymned as "enthroned on high," a "King and Lord" who rules hierarchically over life and death.

The effects of this reversal of Isaiah's vision and of Paul's—as well as Peter's vision of Jesus as a messenger of peace—are most evident today in those former colonies where Christian imperialism, established and consolidated by military power, then turned to the use of economic power to establish what we call modern civilization. Reinhold Niebuhr noted the interlacing of two modern historical novelties with persistent elements of empire:

> Our imperialism reveals ancient motives, but the technique is new. . . . We are the first empire of the world to establish our sway without legions. Our legions are dollars. The primacy of economic power over military and priestly power and alliances leads to the second factor. We are not prosperous because we are imperialist; we are imperialists because we are prosperous. This empire is "economic overlordship through economic penetration."[7]

This does not mean that military and priestly powers are no longer used imperially, covertly and overtly, as recent and ongoing wars testify. The military-industrial complex of the western powers supports an economic overlordship that supplies armaments and technology to whoever can (apparently) afford them. The AK47 rifle is found in jungles and on remote islands as well as in the hands of conventionally conscripted soldiers. The ends and means of this economic imperialism are no longer simply territorial expansion, but terrestrial exploitation that affects the human communities, flora and fauna, soil, water, and mineral resources of countries around the globe.

Therefore the cultural disarmament called for by Panikkar includes much more than military disarmament. Religious and secular powers influenced by Buddhism, Gandhism, or Quakerism are now more committed to the wellbeing of the Father's empire than are major church institutions. The former generate and implement paradigms of peace that resonate with Jesus' blessing of peacemakers. They call for active attention to the economic policies that undergird military and religious establishments, and for personal decisions about the character of our involvement with them.

This is a very different scenario to the one in which Paul reacted to the weakness and powerlessness of God. At that time Jesus' followers were not only politically powerless in the face of Roman military might, but were also its victims and would remain so for some centuries to come. This reality, together with the need to make theological sense of it, is evident in Paul's life, journeys, and letters; predictably enough, it culminates in his and Peter's execution in Rome. The same matrix is evident in the way he used the cultural debris of his Jewish birth and Roman citizenship to build up the potential for new life within it.

In doing so, he gave us a marvelous example of theologic: of language as a response to God at a particular moment in time and in a particular political and religious situation. The power that enabled him to bring about and to express such a reorientation is, Paul tells us, the power of the Spirit:

> For I decided to know nothing among you except Jesus Christ and him crucified. And I was with you in weakness and in much fear and trembling; and my speech and my message were not in plausible words of wisdom,

> but in demonstration of the Spirit and of power, that
> your faith might not rest in the wisdom of men but in
> the power of God. (1 Corinthians 2:2–5)

This "demonstration" of the Spirit and the power of God emerges as the exact opposite of worldly power: it shows itself "in weakness and in much fear and trembling"; as a faith that does not rely only on our strength and wisdom, but both draws upon and demonstrates the power of the Spirit. In all those respects it can now be read as the first, but by no means the last, Christian "opt-out" or "drop-out" manifesto, based on a perception of the God of Jesus that in the twenty-first century is as antithetical to an imperialist mindset as it was in the first.

Such a manifesto would take account of the fact that the former colonialist imperialism has been replaced by the physical and terrestrial exploitation of the neo-liberal market economy. Mercy Amba Oduyoye has described this as a form of "neo-slavery" that makes nations replace food crops with cash crops, receive a pittance for their labors, and then have to use that pittance to pay off debts owed to their trading partners. These unhealthy economic conditions continue to fuel racial, cultural, and religious wars in the economic South while the economic North exploits the situation to keep its arms industry flourishing. She sums up the persistent connection between the plight of women, the health of the environment, and the violence of colonial powers:

> The liberation of women from patriarchy and other
> forms of violence is an inseparable part of pursuing
> peace, and so is the protection of the environment and
> the flourishing of the habitat for life.[8]

This is a contemporary Christian call for liberation from past and present embodiments of the imperial *koinon* endorsed at Nicaea and still active in Christian communities.

For now it is endorsed in the name of its victim, Jesus. It is worth recalling what sort of gathering Nicaea was. The quotation from Eusebius commented on by Crossan (see pp. 96–97 above) gives us some idea of how it operated. In his detailed study of the subsequent disputes over which words should be used in formulating the Nicene creed, John Kelly notes that the actual course of events that led to the formulation is bafflingly obscure, thanks to the absence of reliable and consecutive accounts of the proceedings. Those extant are (a) some fragments of St. Eusthatius of Antioch, (b) some chapters from Athanasius written a generation after the Council and (c) the letter from Eusebius.

Athanasius asserted that the original intention was to express in scriptural language what they took to be the truth about the nature of Jesus, and therefore of Christian faith in him. However, whatever turns of phrase were proposed—that the Son was "from God," that he was "the true Power and Image of the Father," etc.—could be twisted by the Arians (that is, the heretics) to chime in with their own notions:

> In the end, says Athanasius, there was nothing for it but to interpolate the precise, utterly unambiguous, but non-scriptural clauses: *from the substance of the Father and of one substance (homoousios) with the Father.*[9]

Eusebius notes that once this had been set forth, there was no room to gainsay it. Then came the clincher:

> Our beloved emperor himself was the first to testify that it was entirely orthodox and that he himself held exactly the same opinions. He instructed the others to sign it and to assent to its teaching, with the single addition of the word *homoousios* (consubstantial).[10]

What happens when, as turned out to be the case at Nicaea, consent is imposed? Endless bitter debates and schisms arose between eastern and western churches, divided between the *Homoousians* (of one substance-being-

essence with the Father) and the *Homoiousians* (like in sub-
stance-being-essence with the Father). A letter written by
Athanasius late in his life, circa 370, is the point at which
we of the post-Athanasian age begin to see the effects of
Nicaea. The letter begins:

> Sufficient are the writings, [that is, those Western syn-
> odal texts that became the primary source and stan-
> dard of the faith] which Christ granted, the apostles
> preached, and the Fathers who gathered at Nicaea from
> all parts of our world have handed down.

Going on to identify Nicaea's purpose as the refutation of
the Arian heresy, the letter again underlines the council's
completeness in relation to which all other words, rulings,
councils, and parental sources are seen to be excessive and
thereby transgressive.[11]

In her detailed study of Nicaea and its aftermath,
Virginia Burrus notes the strikingly close identification of
the "divinely begotten Word" with the written texts that
now incarnate Nicaea; the linking of Episcopal legitimacy
with an orthodox sonship defined by loyalty to the Nicene
Fathers; the equation of such filial piety with willingness
to sign on (quite literally) to the words inscribed by those
Fathers at Nicaea; and finally the narrowing of those texts
to the key word *homoousios* so that the meaning wrapped
up in it—the begetting of the divine Son from the very essence of the Father—both mirrors and sublimates the patri-
lineal structures in which Nicaea's authority is embedded.[12]

The ensuing history of the reception or rejection of the
authority of this *koinon* and its effects on creeds or statements of belief has led to what Hart calls "the ceaseless sed-
imentation of theological language" and Funk describes as
"the cloistered tongue of the Christianized age." Whatever
terminology is used, this is language that, in spite of being
endorsed by Athanasius as "precise or non-ambiguous,"
requires too much disentangling and so distracts us from

thinking about its subject matter. It is all too easy to forget the inadequacies reflected in our Godtalk highlighted by Paul:

> For the Spirit searches everything, even the depths of God. For what person knows a man's thoughts except the spirit of the man which is in him? So also no one comprehends the thoughts of God except the Spirit of God. (1 Corinthians 2:10–11)

That is the Spirit in which we are free to express as best we may the *koinonia* that has existed between God and the world since "all things began." An intrinsic part of it, as a proper response to the violence of the *koinon*, is a commitment to peace, and through that to the cultivation of unity. In Matthew's Gospel, we are told that this is what makes us, together with Jesus, sons and daughters of God: "Blessed are the peacemakers, for they shall be called the children of God" (Matthew 5:9).

AFTERWORD

God created. Here the shell of the mystery breaks. . . . God's creating is the beginning of God's self-expression.
—Rosenzweig, *The Star of Redemption*, p. 112

God spoke.
That came third. It was not the beginning.
The beginning was: God created.
God created the earth and the skies.
That was the first thing.
The breath of God moved over the face of the waters:
Over the darkness covering the face of the deep.
That was the second thing.
Then came the third thing.
God spoke.

According to this sequence of events, God was not first revealed through speech. From "the beginning," God was and is revealed through creating.

This has significant implications. The sequence and mode of response to revelation is expanded to God creating light and darkness, sky and waters, earth and seas, plants and trees, day and night, living creatures in the waters, on land and in the air. In response, the morning stars sing together, the heavens recite the glory of God, but *no speech, no words, no voice is heard* (Psalm 19:3). Revelation of God and creation's response occur simultaneously, billions of years before humans appear and our voices are heard.

Yet common Christian belief appears to restrict the revelation of God to the *"many and various ways God spoke of old to our fathers by the prophets; but in these last days he has spoken to us by a Son"* (Hebrews 1:1–2). The assumption is that there was neither revelation of God nor any response to it until there was a human ear to hear, a human voice to respond, a human intelligence to interpret, and a human hand to record what was heard. Revelation appears confined to certain times and places in human history, to predominantly male human recipients and their responses.

But the moment "when all things began" is the beginning of God's revelation in the act of creating those things. It is the first moment of encounter and response between living creatures and God. So in the Wisdom writings, Job orders Zophar:

> But ask the beasts, and they will teach you,
> the birds of the air, and they will tell you;
> or the plants of the earth, and they will teach you;
> and the fish of the sea will declare to you.
> Who among all these does not know that the hand of
> the Lord has done this?
> In his hand is the life of every living thing,
> and the breath (*ruach*) of all mankind. (Job 12:7)

In Luke's Gospel Jesus asserted the "present-ness" of God's kingdom:

> Asked by the Pharisees when the kingdom of God was
> coming, he answered them:
> "The kingdom of God is not coming with signs to be
> observed; nor will they say, 'Lo, here it is!' or 'There!'
> For behold, the kingdom of God is in the midst of you."
> (Luke 17:20–21)

The Gospel of Thomas portrays Jesus teaching the same lesson:

> If they tell you,
> "Look! This presence [God's kingdom] is in the skies!"
> Remember,
> The birds who fly the skies have known this all along.
> If they say,

"It is in the seas!"
Remember,
Dolphins and fish have always known it.
It is not apart from you.
It wells up within each and surrounds all. (Thomas 3)

NOTES

Foreword

1. Posey, *Values*, p. xi.
2. Posey, *Values*, p. 474.
3. Midgley, *Solitary Self*, p. 87.
4. Keller, *Face of the Deep*, p. 3.
5. Primavesi, *Gaia's Gift*, pp. 32–38.
6. Crossan, *Dark Interval*, p. 57.

Chapter 1

Cultivating Unity

1. Benko, *Sanctorum Communio*, pp. 79–90.
2. Pervo, *Mystery*, pp. 5–7.
3. Pervo, *Mystery*, pp. 269–71.
4. Pervo, *Acts: A Commentary*, p. 276.
5. Pervo, *Acts: A Commentary*, p. 264.
6. Pervo, *Mystery*, pp. 276–78.
7. Pervo, *Acts: A Commentary*, pp. 273–74.
8. Pervo, *Acts: A Commentary*, p. 267.
9. Pervo, *Commentary*, p. 268.
10. Kahl, *Galatians Reimagined*, pp. 184–87.
11. Kahl, *Galatians Reimagined*, p. 266.
12. Kahl, *Galatians Reimagined*, p. 242.

Chapter 2

Myth and Parable

1. Ricoeur, *Time and Narrative*, vol. 2, pp. 8–23.
2. Barthes, *Mythologies*, p. 109.
3. Burkert, *Creation of the Sacred*, pp. 56–58.
4. Ong, *Presence of the Word*, pp. 19–42.
5. Ricoeur, *Time and Narrative*, vol 1, pp. 193–95; *Figuring the Sacred*, pp. 51–55.

6. Eliade, *Cosmos and History*, pp. vii, 3.

7. Durkheim, *Religious Life*, pp. 100f.

8. Doniger, *Implied Spider*, pp. 2–3.

9. Nelson, *God and the Land*, p. 44.

10. Lovelock, *Gaia*, pp. ix–xv.

11. Midgley, *Myths*, pp. 6–23.

12. Wilder, *Theopoetic*, pp. 74–76.

13. Oldenhage, *Parables*, pp. 82–112.

14. Tracy, *Analogical Imagination*, pp. 276–77.

15. Schmidt, *Basileia*, pp. 9–13.

16. Brueggemann, *Prophetic Imagination*, pp. 34.

17. Wilder, *Theopoetic*, pp. 73–77.

18. Oldenhage, *Parables*, pp. 120f.

19. Ricoeur, *Figuring the Sacred*, p. 148.

20. See Ong above.

21. Crossan, *Dark Interval*, pp. 60–101.

22. Eliade, *Cosmos and History*, p. 38.

Chapter 3
The Word Today

1. Funk, *Language, Hermeneutic*, p. 59.

2. Funk, *Language, Hermeneutic*, pp. 56–58.

3. Robinson, *Trajectories*, pp. 26–27.

4. Wilder, *Theopoetic*, pp. 2–3.

5. Wilder, *Theopoetic*, p. 54.

6. Caputo, *Kierkegaard*, p. 27.

7. Abram, *Spell of the Sensuous*, pp. 243–49.

8. Crossan, *Dark Interval*, p. 60.

9. Crossan, *Dark Interval*, pp. 56f .

10. Funk, *Language, Hermeneutic*, p. 56.

11. Robinson, *Jesus*, p. 148.

12. Wilder, *War of Myths*, p. 20.

13. Hart, *Unfinished Man*, p. xx.

14. Hart, *Unfinished Man*, p. 22.

15. Hart, *Unfinished Man*, pp. 24–25.

16. Robinson, *Q in Greek and English*, p. 103.

17. Hart, *Unfinished Man,* p. 32.

18. Lane Fox, *Unauthorized Version,* p. 154.

19. Primavesi, *Gaia's Gift,* pp. 32–38.

20. Primavesi, *Sacred Gaia,* pp. 126–28.

Chapter 4
Speaking the Word of Life

1. Brichto, *Biblical Poetics,* pp. 68–69.

2. Wilder, *War of Myths,* p. 74.

3. Crossan, *Dark Interval,* pp. 107–8.

4. Dodd, *Parables,* p. 16.

5. Wilder, *War of Myths,* pp. 75–76.

6. Ricoeur, *Rule of Metaphor,* pp. 32f.

7. Wilder, *War of Myths,* pp. 74–75.

8. Margulis, *Symbiotic Planet,* pp. 5, 22–28.

9. Ricoeur, *Rule of Metaphor,* p. 40.

10. de Vaux, *Ancient Israel,* pp. 490–93.

11. Bronstein, *Passover Haggadah,* p. 55.

12. Crossan, *Fragile Craft,* p. 42.

13. Funk, *Language, Hermeneutic,* pp. 134f.

Chapter 5
Encountering Jesus

1. Primavesi, *Sacred Gaia,* pp. 29–31.

2. Funk, *Language, Hermeneutic,* p. 91.

3. Brueggemann, *Prophetic Imagination,* p. 74.

4. Brueggemann, *Prophetic Imagination,* p. 74.

5. Funk, *Language, Hermeneutic,* pp. 138–39, 155–56.

6. Wilder, *War of Myths,* pp. 77–78.

7. Bornkamm, *Jesus of Nazareth,* p. 69.

8. Jeremias, *Jerusalem,* pp. 356f.

9. Barrett, *Gospel according to St John,* pp. 202–4.

10. Pervo, *Acts: A Commentary,* pp. 212–13.

11. Matheson, "Reformation," p. 69.

12. Matheson, "Reformation," p. 70.

13. Matheson, "Reformation," p. 71.

14. Matheson, "Reformation," pp. 71–72.

15. Funk, *Language, Hermeneutic,* p. 129.

16. Ebeling, *Theory of Language,* pp. 196–97.

17. Ricoeur, *Rule of Metaphor,* pp. 33–35.

18. Ricoeur, *Conflict of Interpretations,* p. 384.

19. Ricoeur, *Conflict of Interpretations,* p. 387.

Chapter 6
Earth Identity

1. Ricoeur, *Oneself as Another,* pp. 16–18.

2. Midgley, *Solitary Self,* pp.117–18.

3. Waldau, *Speciesism,* pp. 22–25.

4. Midgley, *Solitary Self,* p. 143.

5. Waldau, *Speciesism,* p. 174.

6. Primavesi, *Gaia's Gift,* pp. 112–15.

7. Panikkar, *Cultural Disarmament,* p. 109.

8. Primavesi, *Gaia's Gift,* pp. 32–38.

9. Primavesi, *Climate Change,* pp. 62–65.

10. Fortey, *Life,* pp. 29–32.

11. Kelly, *Early Christian Creeds,* p. 112.

12. Kelly, *Early Christian Creeds,* pp. 216–21.

13. Nineham, *Christianity,* pp. 7–10, 28.

14. Kahl, *Galatians Reimagined,* p. 92.

15. Crossan, *Revolutionary Biography,* pp. 114–15.

16. Primavesi, *Climate Change,* pp. 113–17.

17. Kahl, *Galatians Reimagined,* pp. 242–43.

18. Midgley, *Solitary Self,* p. 118.

19. Kahl, *Galatians Reimagined,* pp. 23–24.

20. Rossing, *Alas for Earth!* pp. 186–87.

21. Kahl, *Galatians Reimagined,* pp. 92–93.

Chapter 7
The Present-ness of the Kingdom

1. Miller, *Complete Gospels,* p. 285.

2. Funk, *Language, Hermeneutic,* pp. 69–70.

3. Funk, *Language, Hermeneutic,* p. 126.

4. Funk, *Language, Hermeneutic,* pp. 69–70.

5. Funk, *Language, Hermeneutic,* pp. 138–39.

6. Schüssler Fiorenza, *In Memory of Her,* pp. 136–38.

7. Brichto, *Biblical Poetics,* pp. 69–71.

8. Brichto, *Biblical Poetics,* p. 72.

9. Brichto, *Biblical Poetics,* pp. 73–75.

10. Brichto, *Biblical Poetics,* pp. 76–77.

11. Funk, *Language, Hermeneutic,* p. 133.

12. Brichto, *Biblical Poetics,* p. 77.

13. Brichto, *Biblical Poetics,* pp. 78–79.

Chapter 8
Biodiversity and God

1. Robinson, *Jesus,* pp. x–xi.

2. Kahl, *Galatians Reimagined,* p. 220.

3. Waldau, *Speciesism,* p. 166.

4. Waldau, *Speciesism,* p. 170.

5. Brichto, *Biblical Poetics,* p. 79.

6. Crossan, *God and Empire,* p. 15.

7. Crossan, *God and Empire,* p. 94.

8. Crossan, *God and Empire,* pp. 66–67.

Chapter 9
Jesus Tested by God

1. Waldau, *Speciesism,* pp. 166–67.

2. Buber, *I And Thou,* p. 89.

3. Robinson, *Collected Essays,* p. 343.

4. Primavesi, *Gaia and Climate Change,* pp. 123–38.

5. Buber, *I And Thou,* p. 157.

6. Robinson, *Collected Essays,* p. 687.

7. Primavesi, "Ecological Awareness," p. 226.

8. Nelson-Pallmeyer, *Saving Christianity,* p. 150.

9. Buber, *I And Thou,* p. 94.

Chapter 10
Envisioning Jesus

1. Miller, *The Complete Gospels*, p. 134.
2. Miller, *The Complete Gospels*, p. 135.
3. Bonhoeffer, *Papers from Prison*, pp. 163–64.
4. Crossan, *God and Empire*, pp. 94f.
5. Keller, *On the Mystery*, p. 136.
6. Smith, *Way of Paradox*, p. 86.
7. Bonhoeffer, *Papers from Prison*, p. 164.
8. Swartley, *Slavery*, pp. 112–38.
9. Panikkar, *Cultural Disarmament*, pp. 62–63, 96.
10. Panikkar, *Cultural Disarmament*, p. 53.
11. Patterson, *God of Jesus*, p. 10.
12. Caputo, *Kierkegaard*, pp. 46f.
13. Funk, *Once and Future Jesus*, p. 15.
14. Funk, *Credible Jesus*, p. 2.
15. Zimmerli, *Man and His Hope*, pp. 156–57.

Chapter 11
Sacred Unity

1. Robinson, *Jesus*, p. 134–35.
2. Funk, *Language, Hermeneutic*, p. 126.
3. Crossan, *Dark Interval*, pp. 124–26.
4. Kierkegaard, *Concluding Unscientific Postscript*, pp. 194–95.
5. Caputo, *Kierkegaard*, pp. 14, 70–71.
6. Bettenson, *Documents*, p. 51.
7. Burrus, *Begotten*, pp. 189–90.
8. Kierkegaard, *Training in Christianity*, pp. 38–39.
9. Ricoeur, *Rule of Metaphor*, p. 303.
10. Crossan, *Dark Interval*, pp. 86–87.
11. Ricoeur, *Figuring the Sacred*, p. 279.
12. Bachelard, *Poetics of Space*, p. xxii.
13. Bachelard, *Poetics of Space*, pp. xviii–xxxvii.
14. Funk, *Language, Hermeneutic*, pp. 63–65.

Chapter 12

The God of Jesus

1. Hart, *Unfinished Man*, p. 33.
2. Hart, *Unfinished Man*, pp. 28–30.
3. Pervo, *Acts: A Commentary*, p. 276.
4. Pervo, *Acts: A Commentary*, p. 201.
5. Hart, *Unfinished Man*, p. 41.
6. Hart, *Unfinished Man*, p. 13.
7. Rasmussen, "Reinhold Niebuhr," p. 379.
8. Kwok, "Mercy Amba Oduyoye," p. 379.
9. Kelly, *Early Christian Creeds*, pp. 212–13.
10. Kelly, *Early Christian Creeds*, p. 214.
11. Burrus, *Begotten*, p. 66.
12. Burrus, *Begotten*, pp. 67f.

WORKS CITED

Abram, D. *The Spell of the Sensuous: Perception and Language in a More-than-Human World*. New York: Pantheon Books, 1996.

Bachelard, G. *The Poetics of Space*. Boston: Beacon Press, 1994.

Barrett, C. K. *The Gospel according to St John*. London: S.P.C.K, 1955.

Barthes, R. *Mythologies*. London: Vintage, 1993.

Benko, S. *The Meaning of Sanctorum Communio*. Naperville IL: Alec R. Allenson, 1964.

Bettenson, H., ed. *Documents of the Christian Church*. London Oxford New York: Oxford University Press, 1975.

Bonhoeffer, D. *Letters and Papers from Prison*. SCM Press, 1956.

Bornkamm, G. *Jesus of Nazareth*. New York: Harper and Brothers, 1960.

Brichto, H. C. *Toward a Grammar of Biblical Poetics: Tales of the Prophets*. New York, Oxford: Oxford University Press, 1992.

Bronstein, H., ed. *A Passover Haggadah*. New York: Penguin, 1982.

Brueggemann, W. *The Prophetic Imagination*. Minneapolis: Fortress Press, 2001.

Buber, M. *I And Thou*. Edinburgh: T & T Clark, 1970.

Burkert, W. *Creation of the Sacred*. London: Harvard University Press, 1996.

Burrus, V. *Begotten, not Made; Conceiving Manhood in Late Antiquity*. Stanford: Stanford University Press, 2000.

Caputo, J. D. *The Weakness of God: A Theology of the Event*. Bloomington IN: Indiana University Press, 2006.

Caputo, J. D. *How to Read Kierkegaard*. London: Granta, 2007.

Caputo, J. D. *What would Jesus Deconstruct? The Good News*

of Postmodernity for the Church. Grand Rapids: Baker
Academic, 2007.

Crossan, J. D. *The Dark Interval: Towards a Theology of Story.*
Niles IL: Argus, 1975.

Crossan, J. D. *A Fragile Craft: the Work of Amos Niven Wilder.*
Atlanta: Scholars Press, 1981.

Crossan, J. D. *Jesus, A Revolutionary Biography.* New York:
HarperSanFrancisco, 1994.

Crossan, J. D. *God and Empire.* New York: Harper Collins, 2007.

cummings, e. e. *Selected Poems.* London: Faber, 1960.

de Vaux, R. *Ancient Israel: its Life and Institutions.* London:
Darton, Longman & Todd, 1961.

Dodd, C. H. *The Parables of the Kingdom.* London: Fontana, 1961.

Doniger, W. *The Implied Spider: Politics and Theology in Myth.*
New York: Columbia University Press, 1998.

Durkheim, E. *The Elementary Forms of Religious Life.* New York:
Collier Books, 1961.

Ebeling, G. *Introduction to a Theological Theory of Language.*
London: Collins, 1973.

Eliade, M. *Cosmos and History: The Myth of the Eternal Return.*
New York: Harper and Row, 1958.

Erikson, E. H. *Identity: Youth and Crisis.* London: Faber and
Faber, 1968.

Fortey, R. *Life. An Unauthorised Biography.* London:
HarperCollins, 1997.

Funk, R. W. *Language, Hermeneutic, and the Word of God:
The Problem of Language in the New Testament and
Contemporary Theology.* New York: Harper and Row, 1966.

Funk, R. W. *The Once and Future Jesus.* Santa Rosa CA:
Polebridge Press, 2000.

Funk, R. W. *A Credible Jesus: Fragments of a Vision.* Santa Rosa
CA: Polebridge Press, 2002.

Hart, R. *Unfinished Man and the Imagination.* Atlanta: Scholars
Press, 1985.

Hopkins, G. M. *Poems*. London: Oxford University Press, 1930.

Jantzen, Grace. *Becoming Divine: Towards a Feminist Philosophy of Religion*. Manchester University Press, 1998.

Jeremias, J. *Jerusalem in the Time of Jesus*. London: SCM Press, 1969.

Julian of Norwich. *Showings*. New York: Paulist Press, 1978.

Kahl, B. *Galatians Reimagined: Reading with the Eyes of the Vanquished*. Minneapolis: Fortress Press, 2010.

Keller, C. *Face of the Deep: A Theology of Becoming*. London: Routledge, 2003.

Keller, C. *God and Power: Counter Apocalyptic Journeys*. Minneapolis: Fortress Press, 2005.

Keller, C. *On the Mystery*. Minneapolis: Fortress Press, 2008.

Kelly, J. N. D. *Early Christian Creeds*. London: Longmans, Green and Co., 1950.

Kierkegaard, S. *Concluding Unscientific Postscript*. Princeton: Princeton University Press, 1968.

Kierkegaard, S. *Training in Christianity*. London: Oxford University Press, 1941.

Kloppenborg, J. S. *Q-Thomas Reader*. Sonoma: Polebridge Press, 1990.

Kwok, P. L. "Mercy Amba Oduyoye." Pp. 471–86 in *Empire and the Christian Tradition*, edited by P. L. Kwok, D. H. Compier, and J. Rieger. Minneapolis: Fortress Press, 2007.

Lane Fox, R. *The Unauthorized Version: Truth and Fiction in the Bible*. London: Penguin, 1992.

Lovelock, J. *Gaia: A New Look at Life on Earth*. Oxford: Oxford University Press, 1995.

Margulis, L. *The Symbiotic Planet*. London: Weidenfeld & Nicolson, 1998.

Matheson, P. "The Reformation" Pp. 69–84 in *The Blackwell Companion to the Bible and Culture*, edited by J. F. A. Sawyer. Oxford: Blackwell, 2006.

Midgley, M. *The Myths We Live By*. London: Routledge, 2003.

Midgley, M. *The Solitary Self.* Durham: Acumen, 2010.

Miller, R. J., ed. *The Complete Gospels.* Salem OR: Polebridge Press, 2010.

Naess, A. *Gandhi and Group Conflict: An Exploration of Satyagraha.* Oslo: Universitetsforlaget, 1974.

Nelson-Pallmeyer, J. *Saving Christianity from Empire.* New York: Continuum, 2005.

Nelson, S. A. *God and the Land: The Metaphysics of Farming in Hesiod and Vergil.* Oxford and New York: Oxford University Press, 1998.

Nineham, D. *Christianity Mediaeval and Modern.* London: SCM Press, 1993.

Oldenhage, T. *Parables for Our Time.* Oxford: Oxford University Press, 2002.

Ong, W. *The Presence of the Word.* New Haven and London: Yale University Press, 1967.

Panikkar, R. *Cultural Disarmament: The Way to Peace.* Louisville KY: Westminster John Knox, 1995.

Patterson, S. *The God of Jesus.* Harrisburg PA: Trinity Press International, 1998.

Pervo, R. I. *The Mystery of Acts.* Santa Rosa CA: Polebridge Press, 2008.

Pervo, R. I. *Acts: A Commentary.* Minneapolis: Fortress Press, 2009.

Posey, D. A. ed. *Cultural and Spiritual Values of Biodiversity: United Nations Environment Programme.* London: Intermediate Technology Publications, 1999.

Primavesi, A. *Sacred Gaia.* London and New York: Routledge, 2000.

Primavesi, A. *Gaia's Gift: Earth, Ourselves and God after Copernicus.* London and New York: Routledge, 2003.

Primavesi, A. "Ecological Awareness: A Meeting between Science and Mysticism." Pp. 218–34 in *Ways of Knowing: Science and Mysticism Today,* edited by C. Clarke. Edinburgh: Imprint Academic, 2005.

Primavesi, A. *Gaia and Climate Change*. London and New York: Routledge, 2009.

Rasmussen, L. "Reinhold Niebuhr (1892–1971)." Pp. 371–89 in *Empire and the Christian Tradition*, edited by P-L Kwok, D. H. Compier, and J. Rieger. Minneapolis: Fortress Press, 2007.

Ricoeur, P. *The Conflict of Interpretations: Essays in Hermeneutics*. Evanston IL: Northwestern University Press, 1974.

Ricoeur, P. *Time and Narrative*. Vol 1. Chicago: University of Chicago, 1984.

Ricoeur, P. *Time and Narrative*. Vol 2. Chicago: University of Chicago, 1985.

Ricoeur, P. *The Rule of Metaphor*. London: Routledge, 1986.

Ricoeur, P. *Oneself as Another*. Chicago: University of Chicago, 1992.

Ricoeur, P. *Figuring the Sacred*. Minneapolis: Fortress Press, 1995.

Robinson, J. M. R. *The Sayings Gospel Q: Collected Essays*. Leuven: Leuven University Press, 2005.

Robinson, J. M. R. and H. Koester. *Trajectories Through Early Christianity*. Minneapolis: Fortress, 1971.

Robinson, J. M. R. *Jesus: According to the Earliest Witness*. Minneapolis: Augsburg Fortress, 2007.

Robinson, J. M. R., P. Hoffmann, and J. S. Kloppenborg, eds. *The Sayings Gospel Q in Greek and English*. The International Q Project. Minneapolis: Fortress, 2002.

Rosenzweig, F. *The Star of Redemption*. New York: University of Notre Dame Press, 1985.

Rossing, B. "Alas for Earth! Lament and Resistance in Revelation 12." Pp. 180–93 in *The Earth Story in the New Testament*, edited by N. C. B. Habel and V. Balabanski. London: Sheffield Academic Press, 2002.

Schmidt, K. L., H. Kleinknecht, K.G. Kuhn, and G. von Rad. *Basileia*. London: Black, Adam and Charles, 1957.

Schüssler-Fiorenza, E. *In Memory of Her: A Feminist Theological Reconstruction of Christian Origins,* London: SCM Press, 1983.

Smith, C. *The Way of Paradox: Spiritual Life as Taught by Meister Eckhart.* London: Darton, Longman & Todd, 1987.

Swartley, W. M. *Slavery, Sabbath, War and Women.* Scottdale PA: Herald Press, 1983.

Tracy, D. *The Analogical Imagination.* New York: Crossroad Publishing, 1986.

Waldau, P. *The Specter of Speciesism: Buddhist and Christian Views of Animals.* Oxford: Oxford University Press, 2002.

Wilder, A. *Jesus' Parables and the War of Myths: Essays on Imagination in the Scripture.* London: S.P.C.K, 1982.

Wilder, A. *Theopoetic: Theology and the Religious Imagination.* Lima OH: Academic Renewal Press, 2001.

Zimmerli, W. *Man and His Hope in the Old Testament.* London: SCM Press, 1971.

INDEX

ABOUT THE AUTHOR

Anne Primavesi is a systematic theologian focusing on ecological issues. The author of several books including *Gaia and Climate Change* (2009), *Making God Laugh* (2004), *Gaia's Gift* (2003), and *Sacred Gaia* (2000), she is a Fellow of the Westar Institute and was a Fellow of the Centre for the Interdisciplinary Study of Religion, Birkbeck College, University of London.

CPSIA information can be obtained at www.ICGtesting.com
Printed in the USA
LVOW101922160812

294657LV00019BA/178/P